Seals in the Wild

SEALS in the WILD

Fred Bruemmer

LAUREL
GLEN

DEDICATION

For our grandchildren, who, we hope, will inherit the earth, the sea and the seals

Sarah-Maud

Kira-Ann

Renée-Jade

avec amour

This edition published in 1998 in the United States by
Laurel Glen Publishing
5880 Oberlin Drive, Suite 400
San Diego, CA 92121-9653
1-800-284-3580

Library of Congress Cataloging in Publication Data

Bruemmer, Fred
    Seals in the wild / Fred Bruemmer
    p.   cm.
    Includes index.
    ISBN 1-57145-622-8

1. Pinnipedia. 2. Pinnipedia — Pictorial works. I. Title.

QL737.P6B84 1998   599.79-dc21   98-7001
CIP

Published in Canada in 1998 by Key Porter Books Limited

Book design by Jack Steiner
Map created by VISUTronX

Printed and bound in China

98 99 00 01 02 5 4 3 2 1

All photographs by Fred Bruemmer with the exception of p. 23, which is by David White.

CONTENTS

Steller sea lions at dawn on a beach of Marmot Island, Alaska.

PREFACE

I SAT AMIDST A SEA OF FUR SEALS, a vast rookery of 100,000 animals at Cape Cross on the coast of Namibia in southern Africa. At first the seals had been just an amorphous, noisy, smelly mass of potentially dangerous animals. But as I sat in the colony

Those flippered seals, those brine-bred children of the sea's fair daughter.
—HOMER, *ODYSSEY*

each day for ten to twelve hours, studying seal behavior, I began to perceive a well-ordered society. I recognized most individuals in my vicinity, and even gave them names.

The seals slowly accepted me. Over the weeks I advanced from feared enemy, to mistrusted intruder, to tolerated alien. It had taken persistence and patience to accustom them to my presence. Early every morning I drove from my home in the little town of Swakopmund, 80 miles (130 km) through the mist-gray Namib Desert to the colony, where I always approached the same group of seals. The moment they showed fear, I sat down on my camera case. Every hour or so, I moved closer.

One day came that magic moment of beginning trust. A jet-black pup, full of curiosity, waddled up on floppy flippers and stared at me with large, lustrous eyes. A worried mother rushed over, sniffed me suspiciously, grabbed her pup by the scruff of its neck and carried it to safety, as a cat carries her kitten.

Within a week I was able to sit in the middle of the colony, watching the complex interplay of thousands of closely spaced animals and listening to the great symphony of the seals: the calling of females; the lamblike bleating of the pups; the angry, hoarse roaring of the bulls; and, as a steady leitmotif, the surge of the nearby sea.

Each day brought me new insights into the marvelously complex fabric of this seal society. My days were long but perfect: the drive through the morning mists; ten hours or so amidst the seals, watching, entranced, the ever-changing patterns of their lives; the drive home at night through the desert; then a quick shower, for I reeked of seal; a nice meal with excellent South African wine; and a burble of stories about the daily doings of "my seals," to which Maud, my wife, listened with that concentrated interest that masks the tolerant ennui with which wives humor obsessed husbands.

One day, a European scientist visited the rookery at Cape Cross. He and his driver looked for me at the periphery and then, to their amazement, spotted me amidst the crowd of seals. The scientist guessed immediately how that trick was done: habituation and a knowledge of the bulls' territorial boundaries. His Namibian driver had a different, very African explanation: "It is magic," he said. "That man has the soul of a seal."

Perhaps there is some truth in that, for my long love affair with the pinniped tribe began with a shamanistic blessing. In 1952, I traveled on a Catholic mission ship to then still very isolated Indian and Inuit settlements along the coasts of James Bay and Hudson Bay in northern Canada. At Cape Hope Island I met George Wetaltook, an amazingly vital old Inuk (he was then nearly 100 years old) with a host of stories about an arctic world that had ceased to be. The priest with whom I traveled patiently translated these stories for me.

When we left, Wetaltook grasped my hand and spoke very solemnly to me, and yet there was a wicked gleam in his eyes. I asked the missionary what he had said and, very ill at ease (as Wetaltook knew he would be), the priest reluctantly translated an ancient shamanistic benediction, the essence of which was "May your life be rich in seals."

For an Inuk, whose staple food used to be seal meat, this was, no doubt, a beautiful blessing. For me, a budding writer in central Ontario, far from seas and seals, it seemed a most unlikely augury. Within a few years, however, I was deeply involved in the study of seals. It has become a lifelong passion that has taken me to remote beaches and islands in many lands. Whenever I do anything with seals, fortune seems to favor me.

In my thirty-five-year pursuit of pinnipeds, the "fin-footed" tribe, I have also been favored by the help of many people. Scientists have taken me along on field trips; seal conservationists have for many years helped me with my work; friends in many lands have been delightful hosts; and the natives of the North have shared with me their lives as hunters of seals and other sea mammals.

I am deeply grateful to all of them, but the list that follows is, of necessity, neither complete nor accurate. Thirty-five years is a long time. Some with whom, full of that wonderful vitality and exuberance of youth, I went on trips of exploration to the High Arctic now live in quiet retirement. Some have died, but their work and memory remain alive. Many have moved, to other work, even to other countries. I have therefore frozen all of them in time and have given to each the position he or she held when we first met.

CANADA

Many scientists and technicians, past and present, of Canada's Department of Fisheries and Oceans have been most helpful: Dr. Arthur W. Mansfield, Dr. David E. Sergeant, Dr. Thomas G. Smith, Dr. Michael Kingsley, Wybrand Hoek, Brian Beck and Gary Sleno. Dr. Ian A. McLaren of Dalhousie University, Halifax; Dr. Malcolm Ramsay of the University of Saskatchewan; Holly Cleator of Winnipeg's Freshwater Institute; Dr. Ian Stirling of the Canadian Wildlife Service; Dr. David M. Lavigne, International Marine Mammal Association; Dr. Kit M. Kovacs, University of Waterloo, Ontario; Dr. Randall R. Reeves, Okapi Wildlife Associates.

Canada's Polar Continental Shelf Project has assisted my arctic research, and for this I am grateful.

For more than twenty years the International Fund for Animal Welfare (IFAW) has helped me with my annual spring trips to the harp and hooded seals that breed on the ice of the Gulf of St. Lawrence. I am deeply grateful to its founder, Brian Davies, to Fred O'Regan, AJ Cady, Sally Hamilton, Sarah Scarth and all other members of IFAW's staff, and to Telford Allen, expert helicopter pilot and good friend.

I thank Dr. Eugene E. Lewis of Atlantic Marine Wildlife Tours for many trips to harp and hooded seals, as well as to the fascinating world of the floe edge in the High Arctic.

With Jim Allen, founder of Ecosummer Expeditions, I made three extended trips to Canada's High Arctic and learned much about the behavior of walruses and bearded seals. My thanks to him and members of his staff.

The Arctic Institute of North America allowed me to stay at its High Arctic research station on Devon Island, and for this I am grateful.

U.S.A.

On several trips to California and its Channel Islands, I received help from Dr. Burney J. LeBoeuf, University of California at Santa Cruz; Dr. Brent S. Stewart and Dr. Stephen Leatherwood, Hubbs Marine Research Institute; Dr. Robert Brownell, U.S. Fish and Wildlife Service; Dr. Bernd Würsig and Melaney Würsig; and Robert James (Bob) Wilson of San Francisco.

On my many trips to Alaska I often lived in native communities with hunters of walruses and seals. In my study of seals I was greatly helped by Dr. Francis H. Fay, University of Alaska; Donald Calkins, Alaska Department of Fish and Game; Walt Cunningham and Susan Stanford; and Jim Faro. For their hospitality and kindness, I am very grateful to Erick and Fran Keir of Anchorage and Pat Hahn and Sue Greenly of Nome.

FALKLAND ISLANDS

I spent three perfect months on the Falkland Islands. Jackie Draycott of Stanley Services Ltd. arranged all my trips to the many islands with seals. Kay McCallum of Stanley provided me with a home away from home. David Gray of Sea Lion Island gave me good advice. Rob Gill of Carcass Island fed me marvelous meals and let me ride his horses. Ian

J. Strange and Tony Chater, the Falkland Islands' foremost naturalists and artists, helped me with advice and information, and I lived at Tony's home on New Island.

South Africa

I went to South Africa and Namibia with one main aim: to study Cape fur seals. During the many months I lived in both countries I received help, encouragement and hospitality from Dr. Peter B. Best, South African Museum, Cape Town; Dr. Graham J. B. Ross and Dr. Malcolm Smale, Port Elizabeth Museum; Dr. Aldo Berruti, Durban Natural History Museum; Dr. Jeremy David, Department of Environmental Affairs; and Ucki and Detlev von Hunnius in Johannesburg.

Namibia

My study of Cape fur seals in Namibia was made possible by the help of Dr. P. van der Walt, Department of Nature Conservation, Windhoek; Jan Joubert of the Directorate of Nature Conservation and Recreation; and Dr. Jean-Paul Roux, Sea Fisheries Department, Lüderitz. De Beers Consolidated Mines Limited gave me permission to visit the great fur seal colonies at Wolf Bay and Atlas Bay, which are on their property. Paul and Rieth van Schalkwyk were immensely kind and generous, with help, advice and hospitality.

New Zealand

I spent enchanted months with Hooker's sea lions on New Zealand's subantarctic Auckland Islands and I am immensely grateful to the sea mammal expert Martin Cawthorn for taking me there, and to Francis Cawthorn for her charming hospitality in Wellington. Both helped me on subsequent trips to study fur seals, as did Brian D. Bell of Wildlife Management International in Wellington.

A large-flippered Cape fur seal pup explores its Namibian world.

Australia

Australia was marvelous, and so were its scientists and the many other people who responded generously to my many requests for information, permits and help to study sea lions and fur seals. I am grateful to them all, particularly to Dr. Peter D. Shaughnessy, CSIRO Australia; Dr. Robert Warneke, Australian Department of Conservation and Environment; Fraser Vickery and Terry E. Dennis, Department of Environment and Land Management, Kangaroo Island; Mike McKelvey and Dr. Peggy Rismiller of Kangaroo Island; and Sharyn McIntyre of Everton Place, Queensland.

Russia

I visited Lake Baikal in Siberia, home of the world's smallest seal, at a sad time in Russian history. Russian scientists then were scared to speak with Western scientists and writers for the simple reason that unauthorized contact could be severely punished by the state. Consequently my talks with scientists at the Lake Baikal Research Institute were stilted and painful, especially since the state had provided me, despite the fact that I speak Russian, with an interpreter (presumably KGB). No names were ever mentioned; none were written down. So all I can do is thank these nameless scientists, who under such trying circumstances did their utmost to help me.

The Arctic

The Arctic has no agriculture, and its inhabitants, the Inuit (or Eskimos), did not know bread. Therefore, to make the Lord's Prayer more comprehensible to them, an early translation said: "Give us this day our daily seal." They were, in truth, the people of the seal; its existence made life in the Arctic possible for Inuit (and polar bears).

I lived with them for thirty years, from Greenland, across the Canadian Arctic to

Alaska and Siberia, admired their nature-linked way of life that has now nearly vanished, wrote a dozen books about them and their arctic realm and with them ate several hundred seals, some whales and many walruses.

To name them all would be impossible, but I want to acknowledge a few who had a profound knowledge of "the old way of life" and who were kind enough to share their knowledge with me: Inuterssuaq of Greenland's Polar Inuit, the northernmost people on earth, a man of great wisdom and a wonderful teacher. Akpaleeapik and Akeeagok of Grise Fiord on Ellesmere Island, who took me along on a two-month, 1,240-mile (2,000 km) dogsled trip that taught me a lot about Inuit life and was the basis of my first book, *The Long Hunt*. Ekalun of Bathurst Inlet in Canada's central Arctic, proud, strong and self-reliant, who shared his tent with me for seven months, along with some of the ancient wisdom of his people. Billy Day of the people of the Mackenzie River delta, who told me much about arctic life "long ago." And Tom Menadelook of Little Diomede Island in Bering Strait, between Alaska and Siberia, where I lived for six months, who told me the ancient lore of his people, who had observed and hunted walruses for several thousand years.

Northern elephant seal males on San Miguel Island, California, rear high to battle for supremacy.

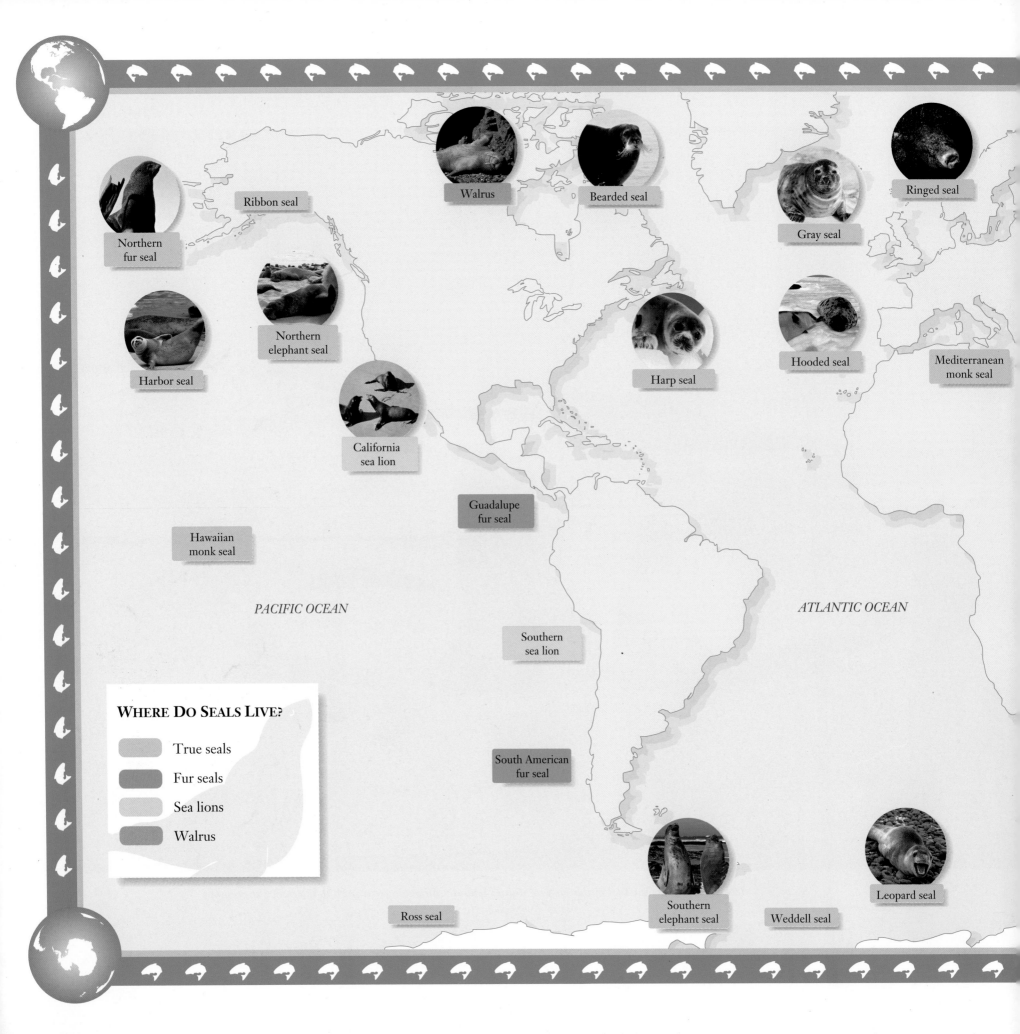

Ribbon seal

Walrus

Bearded seal

Ringed seal

Gray seal

Northern fur seal

Northern elephant seal

Hooded seal

Mediterranean monk seal

Harbor seal

Harp seal

California sea lion

Guadalupe fur seal

Hawaiian monk seal

PACIFIC OCEAN

ATLANTIC OCEAN

Southern sea lion

WHERE DO SEALS LIVE?

True seals

Fur seals

Sea lions

Walrus

South American fur seal

Ross seal

Southern elephant seal

Weddell seal

Leopard seal

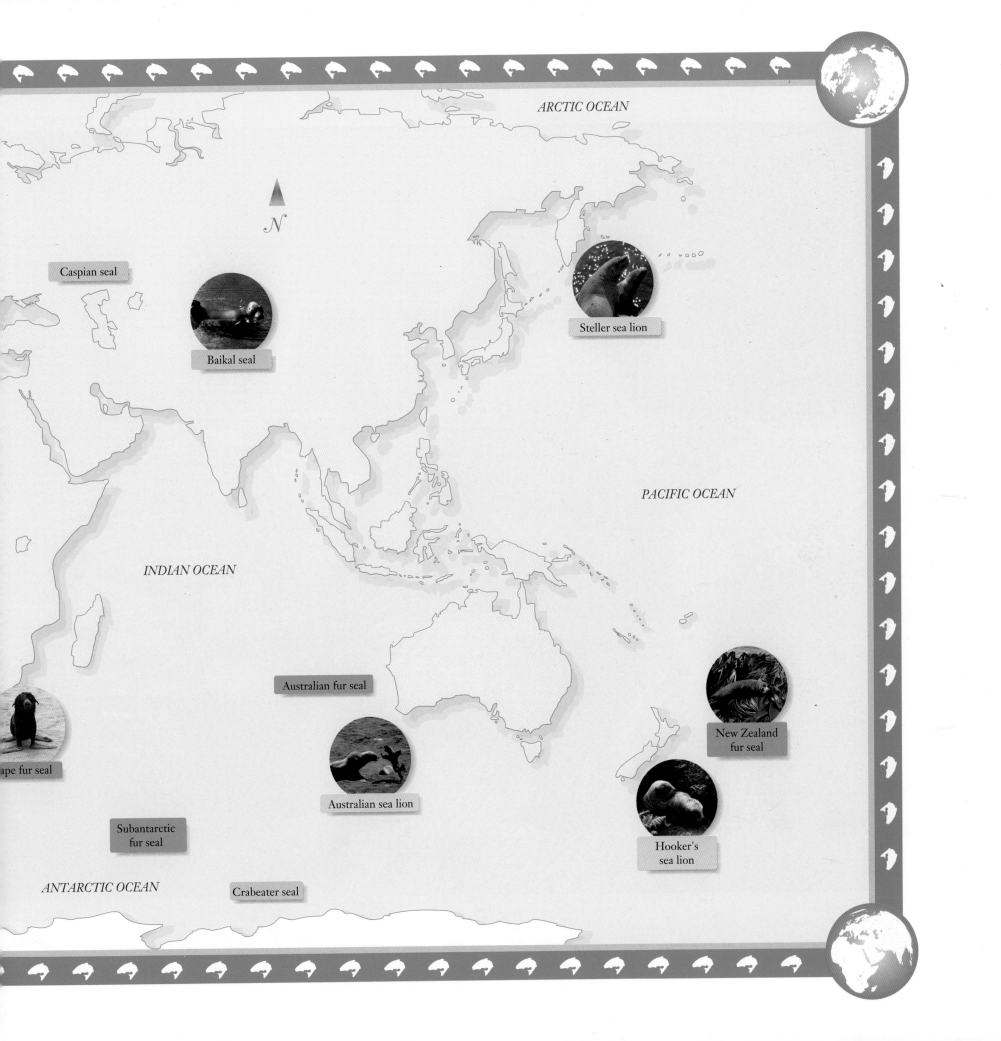

ARCTIC OCEAN

N

Caspian seal

Baikal seal

Steller sea lion

PACIFIC OCEAN

INDIAN OCEAN

Australian fur seal

New Zealand
fur seal

ape fur seal

Australian sea lion

Subantarctic
fur seal

Hooker's
sea lion

ANTARCTIC OCEAN

Crabeater seal

PART I

EVOLUTION OF SEALS

The Calling Sea

HE SEALS, OR PINNIPEDS (from the Latin *pinna*, meaning "feather" or "fin," and *pes*, meaning "foot"), are, as the Greek philosopher Aristotle pointed out more than 2,000 years ago, both of the sea and of the land. They live at sea and hunt at sea and, nearly weightless at sea, glide through it with infinite grace. But they must return to the land (or its northern and far-southern substitute, ice) and struggle ashore to bear and nurse their young, to mate again and to molt.

The seal is an amphibious animal. It brings forth on dry land, [yet lives in the sea] and derives its food from it and must be classed in the category of marine animals.
—ARISTOTLE

Their ancestors were land mammals. With this all seal scientists agree. But unanimity gives way to impassioned argument once scientists ask, "When did seals appear?" and "From what animals are seals descended?"

Most scientists believe that the ancestors of seals took to the sea in the latter part of the Oligocene, about thirty million years ago. It was a time of change. Most ancient mammals were disappearing, replaced by clans of carnivores and hosts of herbivores. The majority of carnivores stayed on the land, but some abandoned the earth for the lure of the food-rich sea.

The late Oligocene was a good time to take to the sea. Currents changed, and massive upwellings from the deep brought nutrient-rich water to the sun-lit surface, food for plankton and the myriad planktonic animals that browsed the vast pastures of the sea and were, in turn, food for other animals.

During this epoch two land carnivores went to sea: a bearlike animal in the North Pacific, ancestor of the eared seals, or Otariidae, the fur seals and sea lions, which have small, furry, external ears; and an otterlike animal in the North Atlantic, ancestor of the earless, or true, seals, the Phocidae, which have no external ears. This leaves the third

True, or earless, seals, such as this harbor seal, have no external ear. The Otariidae, the fur seals and sea lions, are eared seals, for they have furry external ears.

A Hooker's sea lion female on the subantarctic Auckland Islands. Apart from humans, seals have three main enemies: polar bears, killer whales and sharks.

family of the seals, the Odobenidae, with a dubious genealogy, since its sole member, the walrus, has characteristics of both other seal families: it walks on land like a fur seal or sea lion but has no external ears, and it swims by sculling with its hind flippers in the manner of the earless, or true, seals.

In time, most seals spread out from the North Atlantic and North Pacific to the ends of the earth—the far North and the far South. Some species, however, were centrally located: the now-rare Mediterranean monk seal, the Caribbean monk seal (recently extinct) and the Hawaiian monk seal.

During the two million years of the Pleistocene, with its alternate ice ages and warmer interglacial periods, the seals moved north and south as the ice advanced and retreated. Eighteen thousand years ago, at the height of the last ice age, arctic seals lay on ice floes near the coasts of France and walruses basked on the beaches of the Bay of Biscay.

One of the reasons for the great success of the early seals was that they had few enemies. Sharks and orcas killed the odd one, but otherwise life was blessedly safe. That changed during the Pleistocene, when they acquired their two most deadly enemies: humans and, in the North, polar bears.

The discovery of seal images in the drawings done by Cro-Magnon hunters some 40,000 years ago in caves facing the Mediterranean indicates that they had begun to hunt these animals. The enmity of polar bears dates back much further. Some 200,000 years ago during a particularly cold period of the Pleistocene, mile-thick ice sheets spread over much of Europe. Seas as far south as France and Spain were covered by ice in winter. Seals then were common and tame. They had no enemies and basked blissfully upon the ice without fear or worry. Some enterprising brown bears discovered this food source and ventured out onto the ice. In a remarkably short time on the evolutionary scale, the brown bears of this area evolved into white-furred, ice-loving, seal-eating polar bears that ranged as far south as ice and seals. (The oldest known polar bear fossil, a 100,000-year-old leg bone, was discovered near the Kew Bridge in London!)

Scientists may have their arguments about the precise lineage of seals, but no such debates have bothered the Inuit (Eskimos): for them, all seals are the children of Sedna, goddess of the sea. Sedna—or Nuliajuk, as she is often called—is known to Inuit from East Greenland to Siberia, though details of the ancient creation legend vary slightly from region to region. Here is the version told to me by Inuterssuaq in his small house by the sea in Siorapaluk, the northernmost village in the world:

Aglani, aglani—"long, long ago"—there lived a young woman called Arnaquagssâq ("the Great Woman," Sedna's name in northern Greenland). She fell in love with a fulmar, the bird-spirit of the winds, and went to live with her lover on a remote and lonely island.

A year later her father visited her. She longed for her family, and her father took her home in his boat. But when her bird-husband returned to his island and found her gone, he raised a terrible tempest. To appease the furious spirit and save his own life, the father threw the girl overboard. When she clung desperately to the gunwale with her hands, the father took his long-bladed knife and hacked off her fingers. They fell into the sea: the thumbs became walruses, and the fingers a multitude of seals. Arnaquagssâq sank to the bottom of the sea and became the all-powerful goddess of sea mammals, the giver of life.

Killer whales hunt seals in both the Northern and Southern hemispheres.

Polar bears, like this one patrolling Arctic ice, live primarily on seals.

Whenever the seals failed and starvation threatened the Inuit, a shaman would implore the goddess with a magic song:

> Woman, great woman down there
> Come, come spirit of the deep!
> One of your earth-dwellers
> Calls to you.
> Come, come spirit of the deep!

Sharks are a danger to many seals. This Galápagos sea lion escaped alive, but with a terrible wound.

CREATURES OF TWO WORLDS

HE AMA OF JAPAN are probably the world's best professional human divers. They plunge without a breathing apparatus of any kind to collect shellfish and edible seaweed from the sea bottom. Theirs is an ancient calling. They are already mentioned in 2,000-year-old temple manuscripts.

One foot in sea and one on shore.
—WILLIAM SHAKESPEARE,
MUCH ADO ABOUT NOTHING.

All ama are women, and with good reason. The seas around Japan are cold. Women have a thicker layer of subcutaneous fat than do men and it shields them from the sapping chill of water. Whereas men can endure at most an hour in these frigid waters, women can stay in for three to four hours at a stretch. An ama normally makes 100 dives a day to a maximum depth of seventy to seventy-five feet (21 to 23 m) and remains underwater for about one minute with each dive. Most ama begin diving when they are young; a few continue to dive when they are more than eighty years old.

This is the best human divers can do. But seals, which are, like humans, air-breathing mammals, can do much, much better. One adult female northern elephant seal, famished after her long fast on land (about thirty-five days) while nursing her spindly newborn calf to globular obesity, swam far out to sea and then dove and fed nearly continuously. She made 653 dives during her first eleven days at sea. Each dive lasted an average of twenty-one minutes and took her down to an average depth of 1,093 feet (333 m). Her deepest dive was 2,067 feet (630 m). Another female, also equipped by California scientists with a time-depth recorder, reached the immense depth of 2,933 feet (894 m), the dark and dreadful abyss, with a monstrous, crushing pressure of nearly 1,000 tons upon every square yard of her huge body. And the Weddell seal of the Antarctic, while not able to dive as deep, can stay underwater for a known maximum of one hour and thirteen minutes.

To Cope with Cold and Warmth

Each seal is a miracle of nature's design, able to live in two dramatically different environments: it functions well on land or ice and superbly in the sea.

Seawater is about 800 times denser than air (we sink slowly through the sea, but fall very fast through air). To minimize the natural drag of seawater, pinnipeds are sleek and streamlined, their body contours smoothed by fur and fat.

The Greek word for seal, *phōké*, is derived from the Sanskrit root *sphâ*, which means "to swell," and reflects the ancient knowledge that seals are smooth lined and very fat. This fat, or blubber, is the seal's protection against the sapping chill of arctic or antarctic water and, at the same time, a nice, portable energy reserve upon which a seal can draw when times are tough and food is scarce.

The water of the far northern and far southern seas has a temperature of about twenty-eight degrees Fahrenheit (-2.2°C). But thermal conductivity is twenty-five times greater in water than in air. If humans are immersed in such icy water, their core temperature drops rapidly and they die in about five minutes. I know—I once nearly did.

I was traveling by dogsled with the Polar Inuit of northwest Greenland to a remote bay to hunt walruses. It was forty degrees below zero Fahrenheit (-40°C) and windy, and to keep warm I often ran. I jumped across a lead, a lane of open water. The far side, which was underwashed, broke away and I plunged into the water over my head. But, buoyed by the air in my clothes, I popped up immediately.

◀ *Hooded seals—fat female and fat pup, and fat male in the distance. A thick blubber layer provides excellent insulation from the chill of ice and icy water.*

The Inuit acted with speed, precision and the empirical knowledge of endless generations who have had to cope with such emergencies. They yanked me out of the water, as I gasped from the shock of an abruptly cooled body. They set up the tent, turned two Primus stoves on full blast and started to boil tea. They forced the clothes, already turning into ice armor, off my body. A bit more than a minute had elapsed and I was already suffering from hypothermia: I shivered violently (my body's frantic effort to increase metabolism), could hardly talk and had ceased to be rational. The Inuit popped me into a sleeping bag, rolled me and pummeled me to restore circulation, then forced near-boiling, very sweet tea into me to raise my core temperature. Suddenly I began to glow; marvelous warmth spread through my body (constricted blood vessels were dilating). I drank one more mug of hot tea and fell into a deep sleep. Two hours later my clothes had been dried, I was fine, got teased (along the lines "only mad dogs and white men go swimming at forty below"), and we continued the trip.

Ever since, when I lie in March upon the sea ice of the Gulf of St. Lawrence and look down through a harp seal's breathing hole into that emerald realm beneath the ice, entranced by the languid ballet of the seals, so safe and warm in the icy water, and knowing so well my own frailty, I am filled with wonder and awe at such perfection.

The seal is built like a thermos bottle, its warm core surrounded by a thick, non-conductive shell. In seals the shell is blubber. A fine network of arterioles leads through the blubber and brings just enough warm blood to the skin to keep it healthy. Whereas the seal's core temperature is about 98.6°F (37.8°C), the same as in humans, its skin temperature is just above freezing, and very little heat, or energy, is lost to the sapping sea.

Wrapped in warm fur at the equator, a Galápagos fur seal seeks relief from the sun's heat in a rock cleft.

A northern elephant seal bull flips sand onto his back as protection from the searing California sun.

To prevent heat loss from the large, broad-webbed flippers, arterial and venous blood vessels lie close together, like cables in a conduit. The warm arterial blood flowing to the flippers is cooled by the returning venous blood.

The fur seals, as their name implies, favor a different stratagem: they are wrapped in a superb, two-layered fur coat (in Spanish fur seals are called *lobo marino de dos pelos*—sea wolf with two coats) that keeps them warm in icy water. They have an outer layer of long, stiff guard hairs. Glands at the base of these hairs produce oil that makes the outer hair water-repellent. This outer coat covers a thick layer of underfur, its hairs so fine that there are 300,000 or more for every square inch of the seal's body. These gossamer, curly hairs form a dense mat with billions of microscopic air spaces that keep body-warmed air near the body and cold water out.

Fur seals are extremely fastidious about their lovely fur. They groom it often and carefully. Oil spills are fatal to these seals (and to sea otters and seabirds) because oil mats their marvelous fur. It then loses its insulating capability, the vital core temperature of the seals drops by a few degrees and they die of hypothermia.

Sea lions have a single fur coat (in Spanish the sea lion is called *lobo marino de un pelo*—sea wolf with one coat). To compensate, sea lions have a much thicker blubber layer than do fur seals. Walruses have dispensed with hair altogether and rely solely on a thick blubber layer to keep them warm in the arctic seas.

Cold to seals, as to humans, is dangerous, and they guard against it with blubber and fur. Warmth on land can be equally dangerous: humans die of heatstroke, and if a seal's core temperature increases by only six degrees it may die of heat prostration. The large, naked flippers of fur seals are densely vascularized. On warm days these blood vessels

Fanning its broad flippers with metronome regularity, a northern fur seal male in California cools his body.

expand, warm blood courses to the surface, and seals wave their flippers back and forth incessantly, like languid ladies in the tropics, to dissipate heat and cool their fur-wrapped bodies. There is something strangely hypnotic in the sight of a large rookery of 30,000 or 40,000 fur seals all fanning their large flippers with metronome regularity.

This cooling flipper fanning has its limit of usefulness, though. At Cape Cross in Namibia is a rookery of 100,000 Cape fur seals. The coast here is usually cooled by the chilly Benguela Current, which originates in Antarctica, and often the cape is wrapped in frigid fog. But just a few miles inland, the Namib Desert broils at 104 to 122°F (40 to 50°C). Normally the wind blows from sea to land. Occasionally it changes directions and brings with it dry, blast-furnace heat from the interior. As temperatures rise, the female fur seals head immediately for the cooling sea. The pups remain on shore, lean and limp, yet somehow surviving. The alpha bulls, the pashas of the beach, are understandably reluctant to leave hard-won territories and stay until, nearly cooked within jackets of fur and fat, they, too, must seek solace in the cooling sea.

Elephant seals use another method to shield themselves from heat and the searing rays of the sun. They lie on sandy beaches and with their broad, shovel-shaped fore flippers fling sand onto their backs. On very hot days they are covered by a protective layer of sand.

In true seals fur covers the skin and hides the change in skin color from a normal gray-brown to rose or russet when blood vessels near the skin surface dilate. Since walruses have no fur, this color is visible.

After long immersion in the frigid sea, walruses hauling out on land are a pale, whey-colored bluish white. As they lie on a beach on a sunny day, the blood vessels in their skin dilate to cool their massive bodies, and the walruses turn from bluish white, to piggy pink, to russet and finally to brick red.

They Walk on Land and Swim in the Sea

Off San Miguel Island, one of California's Channel Islands, I watched graceful California sea lions body-surfing in the long Pacific swells. They frolicked in the rushing water, blithe spirits of the sea. As the sea rose into a wall of turquoise clarity, they shot through the tumbling water, then raced to catch the next wave. It was a joyous game played by animals in love with motion, speed, the surge of rushing water and their own perfection in the sea.

A world away, on Kangaroo Island off southern Australia, I met less joyful sea lions, the fearsome 600-pound (280 kg) dark-maned Australian sea lion bulls, the Othellos of the seal world. Perhaps because each male has only one mate at a time, the bulls guard their females with malefic, manic jealousy and will try to kill any creature that comes near them, whether a rival seal, a biologist or a pup. They are fast on land and even faster in the sea. All this I knew. What I did not know is that they are also skilled cliff climbers.

A big bull guarded his female on the beach. A fully mature but younger, less massive male challenged the master. The rival was quickly routed and he fled down the beach. There he spotted me. Still seething with fury and frustration, he attacked immediately— an action known to behavioral psychologists as *redirected aggression*: since he could not

Hot winds from the Namib Desert sweep across the Cape Cross rookery in Namibia and the Cape fur seals rush into the cooling sea. ▶

defeat the old bull, he was at least going to tear me to pieces. He galloped so fast I doubted that I could outrun him on the beach. I raced to the cliff at the back of the beach and climbed for dear life. The cliff sloped at first, but then became increasingly steep, the rock weatherworn and friable. The last sixty-five feet (20 m) were vertical.

To my amazement—and worry—the sea lion climbed after me with care and skilled determination. He reached high with his broad front flippers, the soles as rough as coarse sandpaper, found a good hold and heaved his heavy body upward until he found a safe resting place for his large hind flippers, then reached up again for another heave, advancing like a monstrous, malevolent inchworm.

Where the cliff became sheer and unclimbable, there was a narrow ledge, and on this I cautiously edged sideways. That was too risky for the heavy sea lion bull. He glared at me and huffed, his long whiskers abristle with anger and excitement, then he lowered himself carefully and undulated down the cliff.

It is this ability to climb, their sense of balance, their elegance and agility on land, that make sea lions (usually California sea lions) such popular performers in zoos and aquariums. Their reward-induced antics are merely an extension of what they do naturally.

Sea lions, fur seals and walruses can swivel their hind flippers beneath their bodies and walk on them, either in a slow Chaplinesque waddle or faster in purposeful strides, front and hind flippers moving in alternate pairs, as with pacers or camels (like camels, walking sea lions sway from side to side). When in a hurry, they gallop, fur seals and sea lions fast, the massive walrus slowly and laboriously.

Some sea lions and fur seals, mainly unemployed young males, wander far. They

Pink and sprawled, a warm walrus on Round Island, Alaska. Blood vessels in the skin dilate to cool the massive body.

A harp seal pup learns to swim. It sculls, as do all true seals, with its hind flippers.

walk inland and seek rest and cooling shade among high tussock grass or beneath bushes. One eccentric California sea lion ambled up a San Francisco street and ended up in a men's washroom (it was a male sea lion).

Compared with the fast and graceful fur seals and sea lions, true seals are sluggish on land. Spindle-shaped and fat, they dig their short, strong, sharp-nailed fore flippers into sand or ice and hitch their bodies forward, dragging along their rigid hind quarters. This mode of locomotion is called *robben* in German (from *Robbe,* meaning "seal"), and it is peculiar to seals and crawling soldiers. When frightened and fleeing, true seals can lollop quite fast, waves of agitated blubber rushing *thump-thump-thump* down to the saving sea.

Elephant seals are lethargic beasts, conserving energy through inactivity. Much of the time the giant bulls lie on the sand like blimps of blubber. However, when they want to, they can move with amazing speed and stealth, as I discovered rather abruptly one day.

I was kneeling with my camera in front of a globular 300-pound (140 kg) weaner, as recently weaned elephant seal pups are called, and was trying to talk him into looking cute, curvaceous and intelligent. It was hopeless. Torpid with heat and fat, he gazed dully at me and fell asleep. Filtering through my frustration, some instinct warned me of danger. I threw myself sideways and a two-ton (1,800-kg) bull that had crept soundlessly up to me, reared high and whammed down upon the spot where I had knelt a second before.

(OVERLEAF) Joyous Galápagos sea lions chase each other and leap high out of the water in the Galápagos Islands.

In the sea all seals are superb. Fur seals and sea lions swim with their long, powerful fore flippers. Like penguins they "fly" through the sea at top speeds of twenty-five to thirty knots. The hind flippers are used only as rudders to change direction.

True seals scull with their broad-webbed hind flippers. The fore flippers are pressed tightly against the body, where they fit into slight depressions, and are used, only occasionally, to steer. These seals are torpedo smooth: they have no external ears; the female's mammae are hidden in skin slits; even the testes are contained within the body so as not to interfere with the perfection of laminar flow. They swim at speeds of from twelve to twenty knots. Slowest are the walruses; they usually idle along at five knots or less. Unlike most other seals that must catch fast fish or squid, walruses browse on clams and whelks, creatures that are not about to flee.

DIVERS OF THE DEEP

Both humans and seals require oxygen. Seals, unlike fish, cannot absorb oxygen from the water. They must take it with them when they dive. Within less than a minute of submerging, carbon dioxide begins to build up in the human diver's blood, and urgent signals flash to his brain and trigger the alarm symptoms of imminent suffocation. It is an early-warning system, and a highly trained diver can stay down about another minute. By then the oxygen supply of his body is dangerously depleted and he must surface to breathe.

True seals, such as the female gray seal on Sable Island in the Atlantic, haul their heavy bodies forward with sharp-clawed, powerful front flippers. ▶

Seals can take with them much more oxygen than humans can. They have, proportionate to body size, nearly twice as much blood as humans, and the oxygen-carrying capacity of their blood is roughly three times that of humans. In addition to the oxygen carried in their hemoglobin, they store a similar amount in their muscles as *myoglobin*, a protein pigment that makes seal meat almost black.

Seals carefully manage this precious oxygen supply, their built-in Aqua-lung, with utmost care and use it sparingly. Immediately upon diving, in a process known as *bradycardia*, their heart rate slows from a normal 100 beats a minute to as low as five or six beats a minute. Blood vessels to flippers and the outer body constrict. The oxygenated blood is reserved for the most vital organs: the heart, the brain and, in pregnant females, the placenta.

Humans without protective gear die a dreadful death in the deep. Pressure upon their bodies increases inexorably at the rate of one atmosphere, about 14.7 pounds per square inch (10,332 kg per sq. cm) for every thirty-three feet (10 m). At 100 feet (30 m), human lungs are compressed to 25 percent of their original volume. At greater depth, tissues, sinuses, all air spaces, are compressed as if in an all-encompassing vise, the thoracic and abdominal body cavities cave in, the ribs buckle and break, and the eyes are forced from their sockets.

Seals dive routinely to a much greater depth to exploit the fish- and squid-rich layers of the deep. Immediately before diving, seals open their nostrils and exhale the air in their lungs. This reduces buoyancy and makes it easier to dive. It also eliminates the danger that nitrogen dissolved in the blood under pressure will form bubbles as the pressure decreases abruptly when a deep-diving seal soars to the surface. In humans rapid ascent produces the dreaded bends, which are excruciatingly painful and, as embolisms, often fatal.

A Hooker's sea lion mother and pup on the beach of Enderby Island, south of New Zealand.

A blind gray seal mother and her pup on Sable Island in the Atlantic. This blind female returned for many years to the same spot on the island to bear and rear her pups.

As the seal dives down, ever down, on a slanting trajectory toward the eerie darkness of the abyss, its lungs fold until they are nearly flat. What little air is left in them is forced into the tough and pliant, less absorptive regions of the bronchi. The ribs of seals are very flexible; they bend but do not break.

Time and depth of dive vary greatly with different species and with their principal prey. Fur seals and sea lions, which are high-speed fish and squid hunters, exploit mainly the upper strata of the sea. Some can dive to a depth of 980 to 1,300 feet (300 or 400 m), but they usually hunt in shallower water. The bottom-feeding walruses and bearded seals prefer the shallow seas above the continental shelf. They rarely dive deeper than 165 to 330 feet (50 to 100 m). The champion divers are the Weddell seals of the Antarctic, with dives that last an hour or more, and the elephant seals, which can hunt in the Stygian darkness of the abyss, half a mile (1 km) below the sea surface.

When a seal surfaces after a dive it breathes in and out rapidly and deeply. Humans exchange only 20 percent of the air in their lungs with every breath, but seals exchange about 90 percent and quickly reoxygenate their bodies. A harp seal can restore its oxygen supply within seconds after a short dive, and usually within about two minutes after a dive that lasts half an hour.

Most species of seal sleep soundly on land or ice, except those that are likely to be surprised and eaten by polar bears, such as the arctic ringed seal. In late spring and early summer when these small, spindle-shaped seals bask upon the ice (northern whalers called them "floe rats"), they have a very definite sleep-wake rhythm. Typically, a ringed seal sleeps for about a minute, awakes, looks carefully around to make sure no enemy is approaching, breathes deeply and slumps down in sleep for another minute.

*Luxuriant whiskers probably help the bearded seal of the High Arctic
to find and identify the food it eats at the bottom of the ocean.*

Seals sleep equally soundly at sea. Fur seals and sea lions usually sleep at the surface—"Asleep in the arms of the slow-swinging sea," as Rudyard Kipling so nicely put it. True seals often sleep vertically in the water just beneath the surface of the sea, like a weighted bottle. Every ten to fifteen minutes, when the body's oxygen level falls, the seal's brain sends signals to the hind flippers; they then scull gently, the seal rises to the surface, the tightly closed nostrils open, the seal breathes deeply several times, exhales, the nostrils close and the seal sinks again beneath the surface, soundly asleep all this time. Since sleeping seals have the rapid eye movements (REMs) that in humans and other animals (dogs, for instance) indicate dreams, we can assume that seals dream. What are the dreams of seals? We do not know.

THE NOT-SO-SILENT SEA

In the sea, light fades rapidly with increasing depth; there is a twilight zone and then a world of darkness. Light of different colors and wavelengths is absorbed at different levels. Red is absorbed first; at 20 feet (6 m) or more red fish appear black. Orange light disappears at about 150 feet (45 m), yellow at 300 feet (90 m) and green at 350 feet (106 m). At 800 feet (240 m) the oceanographer William Beebe, descending in a bathysphere, saw only "the deepest blue-black imaginable." Deeper still, the dark dream blue turns into the total black of darkest night.

A seal's eyes are miracles of adaptation to the exigencies of two optically different mediums and to the extremes of light and dark. The seal sees adequately in air, and ice-breeding seals can endure the glare of ice and snow. The seal can also dive far down into the sea and pursue fast fish in the darkness of the deep.

The instant a seal dives, powerful dilator muscles open wide the pupils of its large eyes. A film of fine, clear oil, constantly renewed by the tear glands, protects the eyes from irritating seawater, and on land or ice from sand and dust, wind-driven snow and ice crystals. (Unlike most animals, including humans, seals do not have *nasolachrymal ducts* that carry excess liquid from the eyes to the nasal passage. On land, tears roll down their faces, mat the fur beneath the eyes and give, especially to pups, that most appealing weepy look.)

The seal's corneas have the same refraction index as water, and it sees underwater without distortion. The retina is extremely light sensitive, and this responsiveness is further enhanced by the *tapetum lucidum*, a layer of silvery crystals behind the retina that reflect and amplify ambient light, projecting it upon the retina's receptor cells. At depths where humans would see little or nothing even at close range, seals see and hunt quick-swimming fish.

This design functions so well in dim, subaqueous light that you would expect seals to suffer from severe myopia and astigmatism on land and in air: instead of light rays being neatly focused on the retina, you would expect them to be scattered and the image vague, blurred and distorted. But the moment a seal surfaces and hauls out upon the blinding sand or ice, powerful sphincters, circular muscle bands, contract the pupils of the eyes, leaving only hair-thin slits. These are vertical in all seals (as well as in cats and goats) except the bearded seal, where the slit is almost horizontal.

This contraction produces the same pinhole effect a photographer achieves by setting his camera at the smallest possible f-stop so the size of the diaphragm is reduced. It excludes most of the scattered incident rays, admitting only enough to form a reasonably sharp image on the seal's exceedingly light-sensitive retina. Thus, seals achieve the seemingly impossible: they see well in the darkness of the sea and they see well in air, albeit slightly shortsightedly and not perfectly clearly.

It is this slight failing that enables polar bears and Inuit to successfully hunt ringed seals basking upon the ice. Both synchronize their patient stalk with the sleep-wake rhythm of the seal. The moment the seal slumps in sleep, bear or hunter advances. The instant the seal looks up, bear and Inuk freeze, the bear camouflaged by its yellowish white fur, the hunter hidden behind a white, portable hunting screen. At twenty yards (18 m) the bear pounces, a deadly blur across the ice, and grabs and kills the seal. The Inuit of former days had to crawl to within ten yards (9 m) before they could throw the harpoon with fatal accuracy. Today's hunter uses a gun and kills his seal from far away.

Since a seal's vision, especially underwater, is so excellent and seems so essential, it is all the more amazing that totally blind seals exist in many species and appear to lead normal lives. Sable Island, off Canada's east coast, is a remote, storm-lashed sand island, home to wild horses and dead ships and known as "the Graveyard of the Atlantic." There in midwinter is the largest breeding colony of gray seals in North America, presently numbering about 20,000 animals.

In the middle of the island, about a mile from either shore and near the heavy balks of an ancient ship, I saw on my first visit a female gray seal with her pup. The mother was fat and healthy, glossy furred in light orange blotched with dark brown. Her pup, still in

white natal fur, was bulging with fat and content. Mother and pup were a perfectly normal gray seal family, except for one thing: the mother was totally blind, and stared vaguely in my direction with milky-white, sightless eyes.

Nevertheless, she weaned a healthy, rotund pup, mated again and in midwinter left for coastal feeding grounds. When I returned to Sable Island the following year, she was at precisely the same place, next to the ancient timbers, with a brand-new healthy pup. That was her spot year after year (for I returned often to the island). But how, sightless in the immensity of the sea, she had traveled thousands of miles and found the island at her appointed time, then traveled overland a mile or more to her preferred spot, has remained for me a marvel and a mystery.

The answer to how blind seals can exist so well is probably threefold: seals have excellent directional hearing in the sea and hear about as well as humans on land; their *vibrissae*, the long whiskers of all seals, are extremely sensitive to even the slightest turbulence in water; and seals may, or may not, use echolocation to locate prey and obstacles.

Humans hear badly underwater. Sound waves are transmitted through the bone of the skull and reach the inner ear from all directions. Consequently, for us sound underwater is directionless and all-pervading; we cannot tell where it comes from.

In true seals, a few inches behind the eye is a tiny otic opening that leads to the *otic meatus*, the pin-thin auditory canal (eared seals—the fur seals and sea lions—have small

◀ *Sensitive **vibrissae** help seals, such as this young northern fur seal male, to hunt prey in the darkness of the deep.*

external ears but a similar meatus). When a seal dives, muscles and water pressure close the otic meatus. But waterborne sound waves strike the meatus and continue, by a process of conduction, inward through fiber, bone and cartilage, to bring their messages to the auditory nerves. The sound waves reach each inner ear separately and the seal's directional hearing is excellent.

And the sea is full of sound. Thousands of croaker fish in the ardor of mating make a submarine racket that has been likened to "a hundred pneumatic drills demolishing a pavement." (During World War II, this produced a brief panic when the U.S. Navy thought the croakers' love song was the sound of approaching fleets of German submarines.) Shrimp are very noisy: they snap, crackle and pop. Aristotle in his *History of Animals* noted that although dolphins "do not have visible ears, they are extremely good at hearing noises underwater." The haunting songs of humpback whales are now famous; there is even a "concerto for whale and orchestra." The Roman naturalist Pliny the Elder observed that dolphins and seals are attracted by music and will come close to shore to listen to it.

Seals are among the most vocal of the sea's creatures. Sea lions, famed for their lionlike roars, barks and howls on land (a large rookery is as noisy as a rock concert), are equally vocal in the sea. The American biologist R. J. Schusterman recorded "loud barks, whinnies, faint clicks, trills, moaning or humming sounds, chirps, belches, growls, squeals, roars and roarlike growls."

Ringed seals emit yowls and chirps and plaintive puppylike yelps. They have underwater territories, and when other ringed seals trespass, they bark like angry dogs. Harp seals have a gentler repertoire of about fifteen different sounds—lovely trills, a dovelike cooing, sweet warblings and sometimes shrill squeals.

The most melodious sound of all is produced by the massive walrus: the delicate peal of distant bells. When I lived on Round Island off Alaska, home of a large walrus colony, it was strange to wake up in my tent in the morning to the sound of gently pealing bells, sounds produced and amplified by the male walrus's great pharyngeal pouches. Angry walruses guarding females on a floe produce quite a different sound: they clack their back teeth with such rapidity it sounds like castanets. This castanetlike clacking is probably territorial: large males near ice floes with females clack a lot, partly to warn away intruders, partly to impress the females on the ice.

Some seals sing, especially the large bearded seal of the Arctic: a regularly repeated sequence of drawn-out, rising-falling trills, gentle warblings and lugubrious moans, and then the trills begin again—a cross between Stravinsky and Strauss.

A few seals, raised by humans, even "talk"—they mimic human words and phrases. Most famous was a harbor seal at the New England Aquarium named "Hoover," who could utter a few simple phrases and imitate human laughter.

The idea is ancient. Greeks and Romans believed that seals (Mediterranean monk seals) loved music and song and were attracted by it. Celtic lore is full of stories of singing, talking seals, and that gentle monk of the seventh century, St. Cuthbert, sixth bishop of Lindisfarne, or Holy Island, off Northumberland in Britain, loved the gray seals living on the Farne Islands. In the evening he went to the beach and talked with them, and the trusting seals lay around him on the sand and listened. Before his death he made the islands into an animal sanctuary and so they have remained to this day, and they are still home to many gray seals.

There is in this, as in most legends, a kernel of truth. Some seals are very curious.

Unusual sounds—music or whistling—attract them. The pragmatic Inuit use this trait: they make a wide variety of sounds to lure inquisitive seals to within shooting range.

The seal is a creature of the sea; the sea's three-dimensional vastness surrounds it with myriad signs, sounds and signals that, superbly attuned, it senses, absorbs, decodes and reacts to. The seal is immersed in a totality of subtle sensations that guide it and warn it. It responds partly with the innate knowledge of its race, acquired, tested and perfected through millions of years, partly through experience gained in its own lifetime while swimming and hunting through thousands of miles of sea.

PART II

FUR SEALS AND SEA LIONS

◄ *Lorded over by alpha males, northern fur seal females cluster tightly on a breeding beach on Alaska's Pribilof Islands.*

THE GATHERING OF THE CLANS

IPLING'S "BEACHES OF LUKANNON" are on St. Paul Island, one of the windswept, fog-shrouded Pribilof Islands in the Bering Sea off Alaska, still home to vast numbers of northern fur seals. The name, ironically, perpetuates the memory of an evil man, Lukanin, a Russian *promyshlennik* (fur hunter), who murdered many Aleuts and on St. Paul Island killed in one season 5,000 sea otters and 20,000 fur seals.

The commercial killing of fur seals on St. Paul Island ended only a few years ago. (It was a lucrative business. The United States bought Alaska from Russia in 1867 for $7.2 million. In less than twenty years, net revenue to the U.S. Treasury from the sale of pelts alone paid for this land eleven times the size of England.)

The seals were so easy to hunt. They came to slaughter punctually each year, in droves and upon ancestral beaches, according to the millennial custom of their tribe, which continues unchanged to this day. About May 1, powerful adult males, the beachmasters, arrive and establish their territories. About June 10, the adult females arrive, haul out upon the bulls' territories, give birth six to forty-eight hours afterward, and about six days later mate with the males upon whose territory they live. The bulls, after two months of fasting, fighting and mating, leave in August, exhausted and emaciated. Females and pups may linger until late November, when evil winter storms scream across

I met my mates in the morning (I'll never meet them more!).
They came and went in legions that darkened all the shore …
The platforms of our playgrounds, all shining smooth and worn!
The Beaches of Lukannon— the home where we were born!
—RUDYARD KIPLING, "LUKANNON"

The ancient Steller sea lion rookery on Marmot Island, Alaska, vast when this picture was taken many ▶
years ago, is now nearly deserted. Sea lions have starved due to overfishing by humans.

A century ago, safe from lions, Cape fur seals moved from islands to the mainland at Cape Cross, Namibia.

the island. Then the northern fur seals scatter over an immense ocean area, from the Bering Sea to the fish-rich waters off southern California. But next summer all return to the ancestral beaches of their clan, where the black lava rocks have been worn smooth by the flippers and bodies of millions of seals during thousands upon thousands of years.

Theirs is a very leisurely reproductive rhythm. Other pinnipeds are hurried, none more so than the great hooded seals of the North. They breed late in the season on pack ice, a labile cradle: warmth can melt it, currents can shift it, storms can buckle and break the floes. The females are intensely maternal for four days: they pump their pups so full of fat-rich milk that the pups gain fifteen pounds (7 kg) each day. The pups weigh forty-eight pounds (22 kg) at birth, but in four days balloon to 110 pounds (50 kg), blobs of blubber upon the ice. With that their loving mothers, their duty done, lose all interest in their pups. They mate with bulls that hover in attendance, the adults leave and the pups remain upon the ice, living off their fat reserves.

Seals breed at very specific times: 97 percent of all harp seal pups on the ice of Canada's Gulf of St. Lawrence, for example, are born in normal years between February 27 and March 4. In exceptional years when there is little or no ice in the Gulf of St. Lawrence, as in 1969 and 1981, the females can delay birth by many days while they search frantically for ice upon which they can give birth to their pups. They are strictly ice breeders: if there is no ice, they will abort at sea rather than pup on land.

Just as the time of breeding is very specific, so, too, is the area where seals breed. They are scattered for much of the year across the immensity of the sea, with some species making long migrations, yet once a year the far-flung legions gather at their ancestral breeding places.

In fur seals and sea lions these ancient rookeries are often on remote and isolated islands, rather like the place described by Milton in *Paradise Lost*: "An Island salt and bare/ The haunt of Seales and Orcs." Such islands are safe from predators. There are only forty-seven islands off southern Africa and these were the home of Cape fur seals, their numbers limited by suitable breeding space. They could not move to the mainland because there lions and bushmen killed them for food. Now lions and coastal bushmen have been wiped out in this region and the fur seals have moved en masse to the mainland. Today nearly 1 million of the 1.3 million Cape fur seals live on the mainland.

The same thing happened in California. Fat elephant seals made marvelous meals for the once-common grizzlies, wolves, mountain lions and coastal Indians of California. So the northern elephant seals bred only on safe offshore islands. Now that land predators (including Indians) have been virtually eliminated, more than 2,000 elephant seals have settled at the 1,000-acre (405 ha) Año Nuevo State Reserve on the mainland south of San Francisco, to be admired from a distance during their winter breeding season by more than 60,000 tourists.

This concentration of seals on specific islands at specific times made possible the great seal slaughter of the nineteenth century. James Weddell, the sealer after whom the Weddell seal is named, noted in 1825 that "the number of skins brought off Georgia

◄ *Walruses lie tightly packed on a favorite beach of Round Island, Alaska.*

Once nearly exterminated, northern elephant seals have prospered and now have a large ▶
rookery on San Miguel Island, California. With them are California sea lions.

[subantarctic South Georgia Island] cannot be estimated at fewer than 1,200,000." The sealers were courageous, rough and rapacious. ("They look as if they left their country for their country's good," said one explorer who met them.) They roamed the seas in search of seal islands, and when they found them, few seals survived. The Auckland Islands, south of New Zealand, were discovered in 1806. In 1830, the American sealer and explorer Benjamin Morrell visited them and reported with the professional chagrin of a latecomer, "Although the Auckland Islands once abounded with seals, the sealers have made clean work of it." Where once sea lions and fur seals covered the beaches, Morrell counted only twenty survivors. In 1788, sealers found the Juan Fernandez Islands, 415 miles (670 km) west of Chile in the Pacific, and in less than twenty years killed three million fur seals there. Fewer than 2,000 survived.

Whereas some seals, especially sea lions, fur seals and elephant seals, gather annually at ancestral rookeries, others, such as the harp seals of the North and the crabeater seals of the South, breed on vast regions of pack ice, with herds dispersed over hundreds of square miles but, ice permitting, always in the same general area.

Some seals—the ringed and bearded seals of the North, for example—are generally solitary animals and homebodies. They have their favorite bays and inlets where food is plentiful, and there they hunt, mate, molt and bear their pups, never straying far from their home range.

Whether long-distance migrants bound for distant rookeries to keep their date with destiny, or scattered over an immense expanse of pack ice, or headed for birthing caves known only to their clan, all pinnipeds but one have a very precise twelve-month reproductive cycle, during which adults return to their traditional breeding grounds at a specific time of the year. (The odd seal out is the Australian sea lion, which has an asynchronous, eighteen-month breeding cycle. Scientists speculate that this is an adaptation to an equable climate and an impoverished sea. By staggering births, the lactating females spread their demands on the local sea's limited food sources over the entire year.)

To achieve such a synchronous breeding rhythm, female seals should have a one-year-minus-one-week gestation period. In fact, their true gestation period (perhaps inherited from their remote terrestrial ancestors) is between seven and eight months. They make up the difference by a neat biological trick known as *delayed implantation*. After conception, the fertilized ovum divides, divides again and again and then stops. The blastocyst, still smaller than a pinhead, ceases to grow. It floats in its mother's womb, a mote of suspended life. Three or four months later, stimulated by hormonal changes in its mother's body, the blastocyst implants and resumes active growth. This delayed implantation ensures perfect periodicity in pinnipeds so that males and females will meet each year, same time, same place, through all their generations.

Except for elephant seals, true seals do not have dense rookeries, but the gregarious harp seals breed near one another in large herds upon the Gulf of St. Lawrence ice. ▶

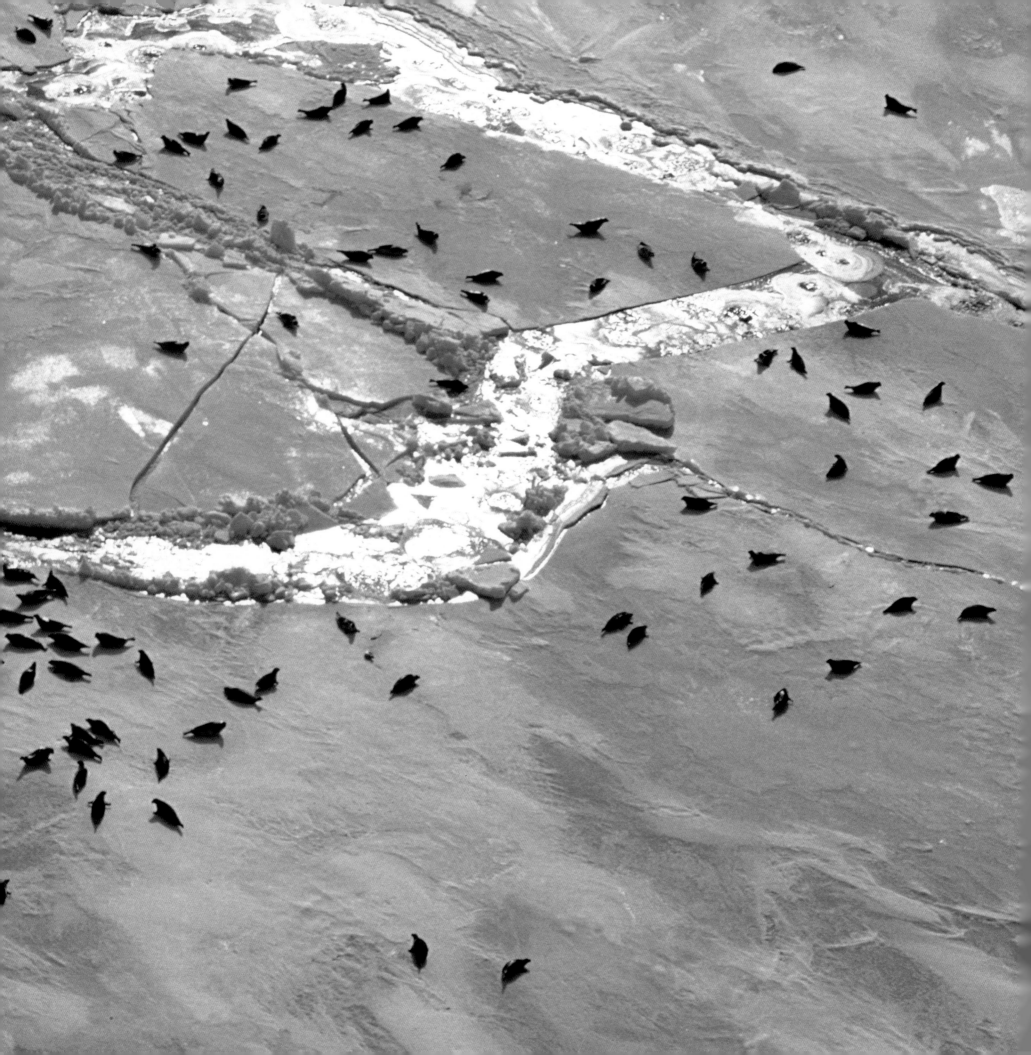

THE CURSE OF THE GOLDEN FLEECE

HEN LORD BYRON WROTE those famous lines in 1817 fleets of American and British sea hunters were already sweeping the oceans of the world and its remotest shores, hunting seals and whales. No creatures suffered more than the fur seals; they died in the millions for their wonderful fur. Between 1792 and 1812, American vessels alone unloaded 2.5 million fur seal pelts at Canton, to satisfy the love of the Chinese for luxury furs.

Roll on, thou deep and dark blue ocean, roll! Ten thousand fleets sweep over thee in vain; Man marks the earth with ruin—his control Stops with the shore.
—GEORGE GORDON, LORD BYRON, "CHILDE HAROLD'S PILGRIMAGE," CANTO 4

The fur seal's long calvary began with the European voyages of exploration and discovery. Europeans discovered fur seals (and penguins) on February 3, 1488, when the Portuguese explorer Bartholomeu Dias, sailing down the coast of South Africa, came into a bay he called São Bras, now Mossel Bay. "Within this bay is an islet on which are many very large seals [Cape or South African fur seals] ... and birds that cannot fly and have the voice of an ass braying [blackfooted or jackass penguins]." Eleven years later, Vasco da Gama, en route to India, stopped at the same seal island, counted 3,000 seals and "for our amusement ... fired among them with our bombards."

On August 10, 1519, another Portuguese explorer, Fernão de Magelhães, better known as Ferdinand Magellan, set out with five ships and 265 men on the first voyage around the world. On September 8, 1522, eighteen survivors of the expedition returned, among them the Italian Antonio Pigafetta, who, fortunately for history, had kept a detailed diary of this epic voyage. It was widely read, reaching, among others, the

Amidst a swirl of seaweed, a female southern fur seal surfaces near one of the Falkland Islands. ▶

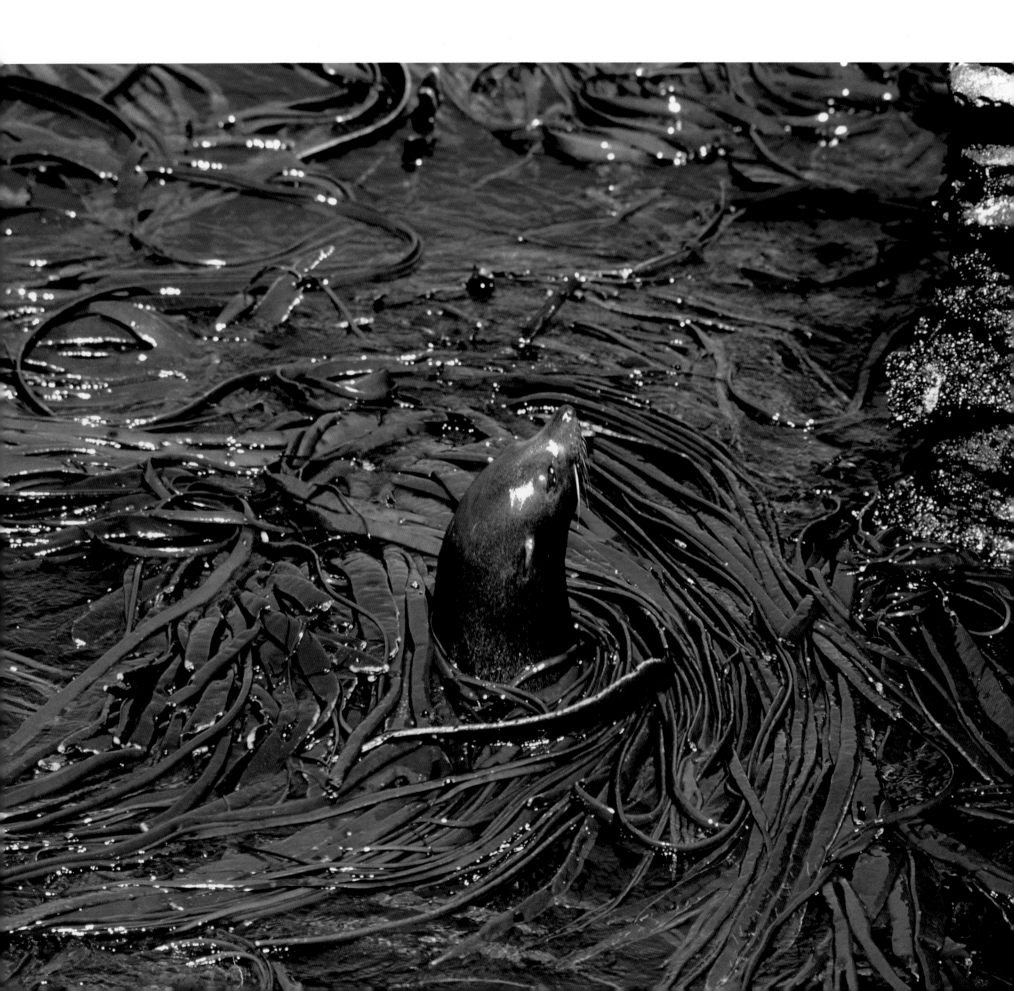

Holy Roman emperor Charles V, a sponsor of the trip, and Shakespeare, who borrowed bits and pieces for *The Tempest*. Pigafetta mentioned many colonies of "sea wolves"—fur seals and sea lions—along the coasts of Patagonia and Tierra del Fuego, and soon sealers ravaged the rookeries.

Two centuries later an English circumnavigator, John Byron, grandfather of the poet Lord Byron and a sailor with a penchant for stormy seas who was known to his (unhappy) crews as "Foulweather Jack," returned with the skull of a southern sea lion. The species is called *Otaria byronia*.

For the fur seals it was a deadly pattern: discovery followed by annihilation. In 1767, the British explorer Philip Carteret visited the Juan Fernandez Islands, west of Chile in the Pacific, where "the seals [Juan Fernandez fur seals] were so numerous that I verily think that if many thousands of them were killed in a night they would not be missed in the morning ... and their skins are covered with the finest fur I ever saw." Twenty-one years later the sealers were there, and killed three million fur seals in less than twenty years.

In 1772, Captain James Cook, greatest of all explorers, discovered South Georgia Island, "a savage and horrible country," but he noted that "seals are pretty numerous." Sealers responded instantly and brought death to the crowded rookeries. "It was impossible to haul up a boat without first killing your way," wrote the British sealer Robert Fildes. The sealers could massacre the graceful Antarctic fur seals with ease, for, as Fildes noted, "they were quite harmless." In a few years they killed 1.2 million Antarctic fur seals on South Georgia alone; soon after, these seals were considered extinct.

◄   *Atop a rock stack in the Falkland Islands, a southern fur seal male and his harem.*

Daring, brutal and brave, the sealers were soon no longer content to follow explorers. They sailed their schooners far into antarctic seas in search of new seal islands, "cleaned" an island and then searched for the next one. The sealers were a secretive tribe. New islands with vast rookeries meant money they did not like to share, and therefore they rarely publicized their discoveries.

When the Baltic-German explorer Baron Fabian von Bellingshausen, in the service of Russia's tsar, sailed into supposedly unknown antarctic seas in 1819, he was amazed, and probably miffed, to find about a hundred American and British sealing vessels there, one of them commanded by twenty-year-old Captain Nathaniel Palmer of Connecticut, who had just discovered Antarctica's great Palmer Peninsula. The British sealer James Weddell sailed even farther south and found the Weddell Sea (and Weddell seals). All the sealers killed fur seals as fast as possible, and Bellingshausen noted prophetically, "As [all these] sealers were competing in the destruction of the seals there could be no doubt … that the number of these animals will rapidly decrease." One ship he met carried a cargo of 60,000 fur seal pelts.

The men moved in among the densely packed fur seals of a breeding colony, smashed skulls with five-foot (1.5 m) hickory clubs and flayed the twitching corpses. Some bragged that they could skin sixty seals an hour. (Perhaps. Norwegian sealers told me long ago with pride in their profession and proficiency that they could kill and skin a harp seal pup in less than sixty seconds.) Skins were salted and packed aboard, and the ship

A southern fur seal male in the Falkland Islands. Once hunted to the edge of extinction, these fur seals are slowly increasing. ▶

sailed in search of another island or, if full, to the fur markets of China or Europe. On the beach, covered with blood, crying, starving pups lay among decaying corpses. For a while there were the raucous screams of feeding, fighting skuas and gulls—and then silence. Another rookery was dead.

It was a worldwide war of extermination of all fur seals, driven by demand for their lovely dense fur (those 300,000 hairs per square inch!) plus the hope of profit and, perhaps, even wealth. About 1740, the Chinese invented a system (a secret they jealously guarded) for removing the coarse guard hairs without damaging the dense fleece beneath. From these cleaned, tanned pelts they made warm, luxurious fur jackets, or used the fine hairs to make the elegant, long-lasting felt garments so highly prized in China. In 1796, an English furrier succeeded in duplicating the Chinese process of removing the stiff guard hairs and Europe, too, became an important market for fur seal pelts.

The nineteenth-century German biologist and author Alfred Brehm (his monumental ten-volume *Tierleben*—"Animal Life"—was the bible of my childhood) summarized the seal "hunt" succinctly: "All seal hunting is mean, merciless slaughter in which cruelty and insensitivity join . . . The oil and blubber, teeth and fur of seals are sought-after articles, and to some extent explain selfish man's mania to annihilate these animals."

How many fur seals were killed? In his book *The War Against the Seals* the prominent American historian Briton Cooper Busch offers an "estimated ... guess": 5.2 million, not counting the legions of pups that, motherless, starved to death on the beaches.

By the 1850s it was nearly over:

Guadalupe fur seal   = "believed extinct"*

Antarctic fur seal   = "believed extinct"*

Galápagos fur seal	=	"believed extinct"*
Australian fur seal	=	a few survivors
New Zealand fur seal	=	a few survivors
Juan Fernandez fur seal	=	three million killed, 2,000 survivors
Subantarctic fur seal	=	a few survivors

Strangely enough, the only fur seals that survived in large numbers were those whose killing was "managed," either by a government or by a state-licensed company. Russia and later America had controlled "harvests" of northern fur seals in Alaska. South Africa regulated the "hunt" and set the quotas for Cape fur seals. And Uruguay had (and still has) a supervised "hunt" of South American fur seals.

In fact, all fur seals, including those "believed extinct," survived the immense assault and slaughter of the early nineteenth century and subsequent mopping-up operations. But where once they lived "in legions that darkened all the shore," as Kipling wrote, only remnants of their once-vast colonies remain.

One fur seal, at least, has made an amazing recovery: the lovely Antarctic fur seal (*Arctocephalus gazella*), named after the German vessel SMS *Gazelle*, which sailed to the subantarctic (now French-owned) Kerguelen Island to observe the transit of Venus in 1874. By the late 1880s, this species was considered extinct. In 1915, a single young male was seen on South Georgia Island (where, a century earlier, sealers had killed more than one million of these seals). A thorough search in 1933 discovered small colonies on several subantarctic islands. All prospered, and populations soared. They reached the

* In Busch, *The War Against the Seals*.

A southern fur seal mother in the Falkland Islands nurses her pup.

A hungry southern fur seal pup in the Falkland Islands calls its mother. ▶

hundreds of thousands by the 1980s and now exceed 1.3 million, with more than a million on South Georgia Island alone, the adored darlings (together with king penguins) of tourists on Antarctic cruise ships.

Two factors favored the Antarctic fur seal: total protection at sea and on its remote breeding islands and an assured abundance of food. Other fur seals have a varied menu; northern fur seals, for instance, are known to eat more than sixty species of fish and squid. Gazella, as the Antarctic fur seal is often called, for its scientific name and gazelle-like gracefulness, has a special diet: it eats some fish and squid, but mainly krill, shrimplike crustaceans that swarm the far-southern seas in shoals so dense they once fed millions of large whales (now sadly depleted) and are also the diet of the misnamed crabeater seal, the most numerous of all seals.

More than two hundred years ago the English poet Alexander Pope remarked, "The fur that warms a monarch, warm'd a bear." Fur seals were widely known by sealers and explorers as "sea bears," and their magnificent fur, so eagerly desired to warm the rich of the East and the West, made them the victims of a ruthless slaughter that lasted for four centuries and on a small scale, in Uruguay and Namibia, continues to this day.

◀ *A New Zealand fur seal male rests upon a bed of giant bull kelp on the subantarctic Auckland Islands.*

A New Zealand fur seal pup on Kangaroo Island in Australia has fallen into a crack between rocks.
Its mother pulls it out and carries it to safety.

SEALS IN THE MIST

IGH ON A LIST OF PLACES with the world's most abominably bad weather must be the region of the northernmost Pacific Ocean. Here, in the vicinity of the 1,000-mile (1,600 km) long Aleutian Island chain, the warm waters of the Kuroshio (or Japan Current) and its prolongation, the North Pacific Drift, collide with the icy waters of the Oyashio as it rushes out of the Arctic Ocean, through Bering Strait into the Bering Sea and Russia's Sea of Okhotsk.

The dry, frigid air masses of the Siberian high engage the warm, humid ones of the near-permanent Aleutian low in titanic conflict. The result, according to the U.S. Coast Pilot, "is the most unpredictable [weather] in the world. Winds of up to 90 miles an hour [144 km/h] are commonplace … clear days are practically non-existent … [and] howling storms may be expected at any time during the year." During World War II, U.S. pilots stationed in this region had a saying: the "Fog's too thick to fly if you can't see your co-pilot."

This was home and paradise on earth to the Aleuts and the northern (or Alaska) fur seals. The Aleuts prospered because sea and land were rich in animals they hunted. The fur seals bred in millions on remote, fog-shrouded, cool islands, surrounded by a food-rich sea and safe from all land predators, including humans.

Discovery was fatal to both Aleuts and fur seals. On July 16, 1741, at a time when New York, then New Amsterdam, was just a Dutch hamlet in a little-known land, Vitus Bering, the Danish-born explorer in the service of the tsars, reached the goal of his sixteen-year quest: *Al-ey-as-ka*—"the great land"—as the Aleuts called it.

Bering looked upon his great triumph with dull, uncaring eyes. Sixteen years of toil fighting the twin enemies of most Russian explorers, hostile elements and the dead, clammy hand of an obstructionist bureaucracy, had broken his spirit.

The return trip was terrible. He and his men were pounded by storms, until they finally ran aground on an island, later called Bering, one of the then unknown Commander Islands east of Kamchatka. Bering died of scurvy, and so did many of his crew. Only one man was healthy, busy and happy, the brilliant young expedition biologist, Georg Wilhelm Steller. On the island were animals no European had ever seen: three-ton (2700 kg) Steller sea cows, largest of all sirenians (northern cousins of manatees and dugongs), which methodically munched seaweed in the shallows (discovered in 1741, they were extermi- nated by 1768); an elegant flightless cormorant that soon shared the sea cow's fate; and Steller's sea eagles, largest of all eagles. There were great herds of sea otters, then tame and trusting, which stared at the sailors with curious, old men's faces. And in spring the fur seal legions came to breed on ancestral beaches, where the dark rocks were worn smooth by their millennial coming and going. The great fur seal male, wrote Steller in his diary, "often has ten, fifteen, even fifty wives. He guards them with anxious jealousy."

The survivors of the expedition returned to Siberia in a boat made from the rem- nants of their ship. With them they carried 900 sea otter pelts. When Siberia's *promyshlenniki* (fur hunters) saw them, their eyes glittered with greed. One of those lus- trous sea otter pelts was worth 100 rubles (then the equivalent of a Russian worker's annual salary) on the fur-hungry Chinese markets.

The *promyshlenniki* were a breed of northern conquistador, greedy, rowdy, brave, brutal, and their gold was furs. There were no ships on the Pacific coast, so they built

◄ *A northern fur seal male and his harem in the Pribilof Islands, Alaska. He may weigh 600 pounds (270 kg), his females only 100 pounds (45 kg) each.*

shitiks, vessels made of green lumber, the planks sewn together with thong or willow twigs, and rushed off to the new land of wonderful furs through seas whipped by dreadful gales. One ship in three did not return.

They killed or enslaved the once-proud Aleuts; of about 20,000, a broken, subservient remnant of barely 2,000 remained. They hunted sea otters to near extinction. They killed thousands of walruses for their ivory tusks. And then it was the fur seal's turn to die.

The Russians were already exploiting the fur seal rookeries on the Commander Islands, the Kurile Islands and Robben Island in the Sea of Okhotsk. But the greatest prize eluded them as yet. Each spring about two million fur seals could be seen swimming through the straits separating the Aleutian Islands, only to disappear into the fog-shrouded vastness of the Bering Sea. Somewhere up there, now that the Chinese were clamoring for fur seal pelts, lived a fortune.

After a search that lasted three years, Captain Gerassim Pribilof found it. On June 25, 1786, the dull roar of a great seal rookery guided him through the fog to a small island, which he named St. George after his ship. The following year on the feast day of St. Peter and St. Paul, he discovered the larger St. Paul Island. Pribilof's first cargo of fur seal and sea otter pelts and walrus ivory from the island group later named after him was valued at 258,018 rubles, well in excess of a million dollars today.

◀ *Near the Pribilof Islands, Alaska, a northern fur seal mother feeds at sea, returns to land, calls her pup, then sniffs it to be sure it is her very own.*

The killing, euphemistically called "harvest," lasted more than 200 years. First Russia and its state-licensed companies exploited all rookeries. Then America and its state-licensed companies exploited rookeries in Alaska. Canadian and Japanese sealers killed migrating fur seals (mostly pregnant females) at sea. The fur seal dispute became a *cause célèbre*: the United States confiscated Canadian sealing ships; Britain, defending the rights of its Canadian subjects, sailed up with the Royal Navy; the Russians accused the Japanese of piracy; and the Japanese were mad at everybody. The French tried to conciliate, but international arbitration in Paris in 1893 solved nothing.

The killing of northern fur seals, at sea and on land, continued unabated, until it finally dawned on all parties concerned that if they didn't settle their quarrels, there would be nothing left to quarrel about. It had been a long and lucrative harvest: it lasted slightly more than 200 years, and in that time about twelve million northern fur seals were killed. Where once there had been between two and three million northern fur seals, barely 200,000 were left. This reality brought about an amazingly quick accord: the First North Pacific Fur Seal Convention, signed in 1911 by Japan, the United States, Russia and Britain (for Canada). All nations agreed to cease sealing on the open seas, and Canada and Japan each received 15 percent of all fur seal pelts taken on land by Russia and the United States.

I spent a summer on St. Paul Island, living with a charming elderly Aleut couple, Sergei and Nadesda Shashnikoff, who spoiled me with wonderful meals and island tales of long ago.

A young northern fur seal male on San Miguel Island, California.   ▶

The weather was mild but dreary: St. Paul has, on average, 200 days of rain a year. It is usually not a heavy rain, just a steady dismal drizzle. In winter it snows. The sky is almost always overcast, the light a soft, diffuse gray. It is a land without shadows.

Yet it is an amazingly rich and beautiful place. Island cliffs are covered with immense colonies of seabirds. The treeless, rain-soaked island is lush and deep green, crisscrossed by brick-red cinder roads leading to the seal rookeries. Golden yellow poppies grow in gay profusion on ridges and hills; entire slopes are blue with lupines.

Every morning I walked through this lovely profusion of wildflowers to Lukanin Beach to watch the fur seals. The great master bulls had arrived in May to stake out their territories upon traditional fur seal beaches. These beachmasters, weighing 400 to 600 pounds (180 to 270 kg) when they arrive, are swathed in fat. During the next two months, they fight and mate and guard their harems (uneasy sleeps the lord with a hundred wives!), and throughout this time of intense stress they do not eat or drink. Blubber, metabolized, provides them with energy and water.

The males, a deep rich brown with a grizzled mane—or "wig," as sealers called it— are long of tooth and short of temper. Rivals face each other, panting, glaring, then strike with snakelike speed, cut and rip. They bleed profusely, roar and snarl, strike and slash, overheat, rest and fight again until the weaker bull flees.

In June the females arrive, svelte, lithe and beautiful. Compared with the lords of the beaches they are small: half his length and less than a quarter of his weight. Some look pathetically tiny next to a top harem bull: he weighs 600 pounds (270 kg), she only 90 (40 kg). Their fur is exquisitely soft and smooth, usually dark gray with a slight olivaceous tint, sometimes a delicate brown. For me, female fur seals are among the loveliest creatures on earth. At sea they are perfection, sleek and supple, they glide with the flow of the waves. On land they pose, with that marvelously artless, artful grace of very refined ladies. On one of the Falkland Islands I watched South American fur seals for weeks. After feeding at sea, the females of this colony surged ashore on the foaming crest of a wave, like Aphrodite, goddess of love and beauty, born of the foam of the sea. They rested on favorite rocks and groomed with care and leisurely elegance, the essence of feminine beauty.

When the females arrive at St. Paul Island, the territorial fights of the males, apart from border skirmishes, are settled. The most powerful males guard the best real estate, the section of beach that, for reasons not apparent to human eyes, particularly appeal to fur seal females (often it is the area where they were born). The females haul ashore on the territories of the beachmasters: some bulls on the periphery have only one or two females; those on the best properties may have up to a hundred.

A day or two after coming ashore, the females give birth to large-eyed, jet-black, spindly-bodied pups that weigh 10 to 12 pounds (5 to 6 kg). After some frantic searching, the newborn pups find their mothers' teats and with blissful urgency suckle the cream-thick milk that contains 41 percent fat and 14 percent protein.

Rookery life seems constant chaos. The females may be lovely and gregarious, but crowded together they are an ill-tempered, snarly lot, forever bickering with one another. The great males are busy. When a female moves toward the edge of a bull's territory, he rushes over, scattering females, steamrollers squalling pups, blocks the straying female's path, barks angrily at her, his normally droopy Genghis Khan whiskers abristle, and shakes his head vigorously. He may pick her up by the loose back skin and with one mighty swing toss her back into the center of his harem. The females tend to look demure and adoring—then sneak off the moment the pasha's back is turned.

About six days after giving birth, the females mate with their territorial male, and soon after they go to sea to feed. The pups begin to form pup pods at the edge of the harum-scarum of the rookeries with those rushing, crushing bulls. When a female returns, she pauses at the sea edge and calls loudly. Amidst that vast chorus of cries and

roars and whimpers, her pup hears her and bleats eagerly and loudly. The mother comes, sniffs the pup to make sure it is her very own (for she will never feed another pup), and her happy, hungry pup begins to nurse.

In the vicinity of the rookeries, but at a respectful distance from the belligerent territorial bulls, the immature males haul out in big, chummy groups, from a few hundred to well over a thousand. In the past it was they, the surplus males of this polygamous seal society, who were killed by seal hunters. The daily drive to death by clubbing was still carried out when I lived on St. Paul Island.

Every morning (except Sundays) in the chill hours before dawn, from June 26 until the end of July, Aleut sealers drove in trucks to one of the rookeries. Fast and noiselessly, they ran between seals and beach and herded the bachelors very slowly inland, pausing periodically so that the seals would not overheat (if seals die of heat prostration it affects the quality of their pelts). On level, grassy ground beyond each rookery was a killing field. *Ungisxalgaq*, the Aleuts called it, "the place without hope."

The great commercial kills have ended, but the number of northern fur seals keeps declining. Most scientists believe that ruthless overfishing by the fleets of many nations in the once immensely fish-rich Bering Sea is the major cause for this decline (and the much more drastic decline of Steller, or northern, sea lions living in the same region). A major food fish of both species, the walleye pollock, has recently become a top prey of commercial fishermen: their catch has soared from zero in 1950 to more than two million tons annually. Deprived of food, fur seals and sea lions die.

◀ *Skinned carcasses lie upon the lush green sward of the Pribilof Islands. In the distance, other herds of northern fur seals are driven to the ancient "killing fields." This hunt has now ceased.*

A few of these fur seals have moved from their ancient home islands far in the northern mists to the sunny beaches of California. In 1968, three American scientists, Burney J. LeBoeuf, Richard S. Petersen and Robert L. DeLong, found a breeding colony of 100 northern fur seals on San Miguel, one of California's Channel Islands, which happens to lie directly in the path of the cold (and food-rich) California Current and thus suits the thick-furred northern fur seals. This group has slowly increased to about 2,000 animals, a fascinating modern example of seal dispersal and colonization (long ago, some far-roving California sea lions discovered the Galápagos Islands, liked them and settled there, and their descendants are now Galápagos sea lions, a subspecies of the California sea lion).

On St. Paul Island, the mighty males, their duty done (top males may have sired 100 future pups) begin to leave the rookeries at the end of July. The great bulls that arrived in late May so fat and feisty are thin and spent and worn, their once-glossy coats dull and drab. They swim far out into the Bering Sea to feed intensively and restore their depleted fat reserves.

Females, pups and bachelor bulls remain. The females stay longer and longer at sea to return with more fat-rich milk for their increasingly active, fast-growing pups. Content at first to sleep, between meals, in densely clustered piles, the pups now become inquisitive and venturesome. Water fascinates them and frightens them. They waddle down to the sea, then scamper frantically up the beach when they get splashed by a wave. Curiosity wins. They begin to play in rock pools, chase one another, and build up strength and skill.

By November, the mother-pup bond weakens. The pups of fur seals in more temperate climates often stay with their mothers for a year and sometimes longer (it is quite common to see a Galápagos fur seal mother nurse both her recently born pup and its hefty last year's sibling). But the pups of the antarctic fur seal of the far South and the northern fur seal are fed often, grow fast and fat and are weaned before their mothers leave the rookeries.

As the storms of early winter scream across the northern isles, the last females, pups and bachelor bulls leave the dark lava beaches. The ancient rookeries are silent until next May, when the great males return to fight, to mate, to perpetuate the cycle of fur seal life.

OF DIAMONDS AND SEALS

FUR SEALS EVOLVED about twelve million years ago in the northern Pacific, their thick, dense fur waterproof and marvelously warm, perfect for a chilly land and a frigid sea. But they spread from their northern haunts: only the northern fur seals remain on the ancestral range of their race; all other fur seals moved south. Some—the antarctic and subantarctic fur seals—found living conditions similar to those of their remote ancestors in the far North. The New Zealand and Australian fur seals settled on cool coasts and near cold sea currents. But a few took up residence in hot regions: the Cape fur seals in southern Africa and the Galápagos fur seals, still wrapped in that marvelously thick fur, beneath the searing sun of the equator. A fur coat in the tropics, though elegant, can be dangerously warm.

The Galápagos sea lions, as the German scientist Fritz Trillmich, who studied the seals of these islands for more than ten years, has noted, "have found an elegant solution to the problem of heat stress": they live at the edge of sheltered lagoons, where any hot mother or pup can safely go into the water for a cooling dip. And the big fat males, rather than defend hot lava-rock territories, swim along their section of beach, back and forth. There they bellow fiercely, fight rivals in the water and cool off after mating. Most Galápagos sea lions also feed during the day and stay ashore during the cool of the night.

The much more densely furred Galápagos fur seals feed at night and stay ashore during the heat of the day. They, too, live near surf-swept capes—dangerous places for pups, which can quickly die in the tossing waves. Because the pups are small, they can find cooling shade in nooks and crannies. Some mothers commute. They nurse their pups, then seek solace in the cooling sea. A few lie on wave-washed rock ledges. And a fortunate few

A Cape fur seal male and his harem rest on wave-sculpted rocks at Cape Cross in Namibia.

lie in cool, wave-carved, seal-length niches in the rock face near the sea, places that are in great demand and are normally occupied by females of high social status.

The Cape fur seals of southern Africa, as we have seen, lived originally on most of the forty-seven islands off this coast but not on the mainland, where they were easy prey for lions and Strandloper Bushmen, a now-extinct group of Bushmen who lived along the sea. On the islands, washed by the chilly Benguela Current, which originates in Antarctica, the fur seals were safe from land predators and pleasantly cool. But living space was at a premium and colonies could not expand, thus population growth was limited.

Once lions and bushmen were gone, both victims of European colonizers, the fur seals could move from their cramped islands to the limitless mainland. The first mainland fur seal colony formed at Cape Cross in today's Namibia, probably in the 1850s. The seals occupied first the rocky, island-like promontory that is the cape, prospered and spread. The rookery of more than 100,000 animals now stretches about two miles (3 km) along the beach.

They, too, have a heat problem. Normally this coast, thanks to the frigid (and fish-rich) Benguela Current, is cool and foggy, conditions that appeal to fur-wrapped seals. But occasionally the wind veers and brings with it the broiling heat from the Namib Desert, just inland from the coast.

I spent entranced months at this colony, accepted by the seals, sitting in their midst, always with the same group. I knew every male, female and pup, the extent of each male's territory and the number of females in his harem. The pups would waddle over to nuzzle me, curious but no longer afraid. Scientists call this *habituation*; it is my favorite

Svelte and elegant, a Cape fur seal female at the Cape Cross rookery in Namibia.

approach to the study of seal behavior because it removes that inhibiting barrier of fear or animosity that normally divides humans from seals.

A vast rookery like this is constant motion and commotion. Despite appearances, though, it is not chaotic but a well-ordered seal society. Males upon this featureless sand beach have strictly delineated and well-known territories won in hard fights at the beginning of the breeding season. Neighboring bulls know these invisible borders with total certainty: they advance to their territorial boundary line and growl and hurl threats at each other, but neither male will put one big flipper across the border because that would be a *casus belli*—a call to war—and lead to an immediate fight, something both males want to avoid because they cannot afford this additional drain on their energy reserves.

The females, once mated, leave freely to feed at sea. Their pups gather in pods at the edge of the rookery, piles of coal-black youngsters, gaining warmth and reassurance from close contact with one another.

The mothers, after feeding and replenishing their own energy reserves and the milk supplies for their pups, land near their bull's territory and call, loud and insistently. When 5,000 landing mothers call, it is a mighty chorus, yet each call is distinct, known to one particular pup, and that pup responds instantly, for that call means milk. The pup bleats loudly, shrilly, and again 5,000 bleating pups are a discordant chorus, yet each mother recognizes the call of her pup and ignores all others. Calling to each other, mother and pup are soon reunited. The mother sniffs her pup to make absolutely sure it is her own, lies on her side, and the pup begins to nurse.

◀   *Cape fur seals mate upon the Cape Cross beach in Namibia.*

This pattern is abruptly broken when a heat wave from the nearby Namib Desert hits the beach. The females leave immediately. Bachelor bulls follow quickly. The territorial bulls linger on their hard-won territories as long as possible, but then they, too, must cool in the sea. Their normal core body temperature is about 98.6°F (37.8°C). If it rises by only six degrees, the heat can kill them.

Finally on this particular day during my visit of several months, the blazing beach was nearly empty. Where the great rookery had stretched like a dark band upon the yellow sand for two miles (3 km), only the pups remained, now scattered, suffering but surviving. A few panting jackals ate dead pups and placentae, and I sat, amidst pups, jackals and stench, upon my camera case, torpid in the crushing heat.

Eventually the wind changed, and cool ocean air flowed again over the beach. The seals came ashore, and then it was fascinating to see with what precision 100,000 returning seals reestablished territories on that seemingly uniform sand beach. The entire complex mosaic of territories was re-created with great exactitude, the way a milling audience returns to their seats after an intermission at the opera. Since the bulls established hierarchical standing and territories early in the season, reconquering the territories after each heat wave would put an intolerable strain on the animals, for they have already been severely stressed by fasting, fighting, mating and periods of sizzling heat. Hence the strict adherence to the *status quo ante*.

As the Cape fur seals spread from offshore islands to the mainland, they acquired a mighty protector, De Beers Consolidated Mines, the world's foremost producer of gem diamonds.

In April 1908, when today's Namibia was a German colony, Zacharias Lewala, a native worker, gave his boss, the German railroad inspector August Stauch, a strange pebble he had found near the railroad track at Kolmanskop, a few miles inland from the coastal town of Lüderitz. It was a diamond. Shortly after, Stauch and two companions made a prospecting trip. In a letter now preserved in the Lüderitz Museum, one of them wrote to relatives in Germany that they had gone far into the desert and were short of provisions, when, late one evening, they came into a *Märchental*—an "enchanted valley." As they ate their frugal meal, the moon rose—*und im Mondlicht glitzerten die Diamanten*—"and the diamonds glittered in the moonlight."

They filled pouches, pockets and bags with diamonds and walked back to Lüderitz. All three, of course, were now immensely wealthy, but they wanted to be wealthier. Well provisioned and equipped with large bags, they rushed back to the enchanted valley. But it had vanished. In their absence, the valley and the diamonds had been buried, obliterated by the shifting sands of the desert.

These reports naturally resulted in a diamond rush, a free-for-all that did not suit the German colonial authorities. They assigned to the Deutsche Kolonial-Gesellschaft für Südwestafrika exclusive mining rights in the 21,182 square miles (54,861 sq. km) *Sperrgebiet*, "forbidden region," which was soon hemmed by signs that said *Verboten!*

After World War I, De Beers acquired the diamond rights and the *Sperrgebiet* became its fief. Sometime in the 1940s, the fur seals settled there. Rarely disturbed, they increased rapidly. At Wolf Bay and nearby Atlas Bay, some 380,000 seals live in the restricted area, a diamond-rich coastal zone nearly twice the size of Belgium.

Surrounded by diamonds, the fur seals are left to pup in peace. The largest mainland fur seal colony, with a peak population of 360,000 animals, is at Kleinsee in South Africa's Namaqualand, another diamond region controlled by De Beers. It is off-limits to the general public, and a haven for fur seals. In southern Africa, diamonds are a seal's best friend.

Love in the fur seal world. A Cape fur seal male sniffs a female on a rock above the sea in Namibia. ▶

Lions of the Sea

HE "SEALS" CHARLES DARWIN SAW on January 1, 1835, on the coast of Chile were southern sea lions, and they were unusually somnolent and quiet. Normally, most sea lions roar (California sea lions bark!); to that and to the luxuriant manes of the males of some species, especially the southern sea lions, they owe their name. The famous Russian author (and physician) Anton Chekhov spent several months in 1890 on Sakhalin Island off Siberia (mainly to study the lives of convicts and alleviate their fate by treating the sick and urging authorities to improve conditions). There a great crag called Dangerous Rock was covered with Steller sea lions: "The roaring of this enormous wild herd astounded us," wrote Chekhov.

The number of seals which we saw was quite astonishing: every bit of flat rock, and parts of the beach, were covered with them. They appeared to be of a loving disposition, and lay huddled together, fast asleep . . ."
—CHARLES DARWIN, THE VOYAGE OF THE BEAGLE

Fur seals are svelte, sleek and densely furred, and were once very valuable. Sea lions are more massive—a great Steller sea lion bull is thirteen feet (4 m) long and can weigh more than a ton—have a coarser, one-layer fur coat, are fatter than fur seals, of limited commercial value, but are hated by fishermen as competitors. Until recently, Oregon authorities paid a $10 bounty for each sea lion killed; along the coast of British Columbia nearly two-thirds of the province's 12,000 sea lions were shot over a number of years; and after bitter complaints by Japanese fishermen, Steller sea lions were attacked by aircraft on Hokkaido Island on March 23, 1959.

Such assaults have ceased, but sea lion poaching is common. When I visited the California Marine Mammal Center at Fort Mason, across the Golden Gate Bridge from San Francisco, most of its "guests" were wounded sea lions found on the beaches. Dead sea lions, shot by vengeful fishermen, simply sink and vanish. A few years ago I spent some winter weeks on Hokkaido Island with Japan's famous nature photographer Akira Uchiyama, and he showed me many restaurants in coastal towns that had Steller sea lion meat on the menu. Fishermen shoot them and sell them.

To two native populations, one of the far South, the other of the far North, sea lions were of great importance. Two of the now-extinct Fuegian tribes of Tierra del Fuego hunted southern sea lions. The Yahgans and Alacalufs, known as the "Canoe Indians," were a coastal people who traveled widely in bark canoes and lived primarily on fish, shellfish, sea lions and some fur seals. They ate the seals but, oddly enough, disdained to dress in fine furs. Despite the miserable climate—cold, moist and nearly always windy—they wore hardly any clothing.

To Alaska's Aleuts, the Steller sea lion was a mainstay of their existence on the 1,000 mile (1,600 km) long, rain and wind-haunted island chain they inhabited. (I once lived on Attu, westernmost of these islands; it has, on average, only five clear days a year!)

Sea lion flesh, fresh or dried, was the Aleuts' staple food. The high-calorie blubber was eaten with lean meat or rendered into oil for their lamps. From the hide they made ropes, harpoon lines and the covers for their baidars and baidarkas, their superbly sea-worthy kayaks and large open boats. The bones were used: ribs were made into tools to dig up the edible corms and roots of plants; the humerus they fashioned into a strong club; and the baculum, the penis bone, became a flaker to make stone blades. Teeth were filed into pendants or made into fishhooks. The long whiskers decorated their hunting hats. Sea lion sinew was their thread and was also used to make cordage. The skins of the rough-soled flippers were made into long-lasting, skidproof boot soles. From the heart sac, they made water bottles; from the esophagus, waterproof boot leggings and pouches. In dried seal stomachs they preserved their salmon catch. They carefully removed the Steller sea lion's long intestine (about 264 feet [80 m] in length, still short compared with the 656 foot [200 m] long gut of a southern elephant seal!). Then they washed it, split it, dried it and made from it their superb *kamleikas*, waterproof parkas that weighed less than a pound and were essential garments for these hunters of the stormy seas.

Sea lions, initially, were handy meals for hungry European explorers. Being short of food near Tierra del Fuego in 1578, the crew of Sir Francis Drake, the first Englishman to circumnavigate the world, "Kylled some seyles [southern sea lions] for owr provysy-on." On Kangaroo Island off southern Australia, the explorer Matthew Flinders tackled the fast, aggressive Australian sea lions and nearly lost a sailor in April 1802. He noted wryly that "Richard Stanley … having been simple enough to attack a large seal with a small stick … was seized upon by the seal and much bitten in the leg … [and will be for-ever] lame from it."

By the mid nineteenth century, sea hunters had eliminated many of the most valu-able marine mammals: sea otters were nearly extinct; several fur seal species were near the edge. Sea lions, of course, were not nearly as valuable, but they were numerous and could be turned into oil or glue. The American sealer-whaler-naturalist-writer Charles M. Scammon said a large Steller sea lion bull yielded forty gallons (151 l) of oil, though ten to fifteen gallons (38 to 57 l) per bull was the usual yield. More valuable than the low-quality oil, said Scammon, were the sea lion hides, which in the 1850s were used "as glue-stock."

The upper lip of the Steller sea lion (as, indeed, of all sea lions) has long white or yellowish whiskers, about thirty-four on each side, with the longest eighteen inches

*The Hooker's sea lion, rarest of all sea lions, and the yellow-eyed penguin, rarest of all penguins,
meet on the subantarctic Auckland Islands of New Zealand.*

A young Hooker's sea lion "beach bull" tries to mate with a fighting female in the Auckland Islands surf. She easily repels him.

(46 cm) in length. Flexible and strong, these whiskers were greatly in demand in China: they were perfect for cleaning opium pipes.

The hunt was simple and brutal. The hunters, wrote Scammon, "landed some distance from the rookery, then cautiously advanced, and suddenly, yelling, and flourishing muskets, clubs and lances, rushed up within a few yards of them, while the pleading creatures … were quite overcome with dismay and remained nearly motionless" and were easily butchered. (Anton Chekhov, speaking about the convicts on Sakhalin Island, argued, with some irony, that they should never be employed in the fur seal killing. "When they [the fur seal hunters] slaughter the sea bears with cudgels, their brains spatter on all sides and the eyes of the poor creatures jump out of their sockets. The exiles, especially those sent there for murder, should not be permitted to participate in similar spectacles.")

In Scammon's time, as in ours, the main incentive to kill sea lions (and other seals) was what were then coyly called "the trimmings," the genitalia of sea lion males that in the 1850s found an eager "market in China" as an ancient, useless but nevertheless valuable aphrodisiac. The demand continues and today is the main reason for the continued killing of harp seals in Canada and the resumption of fur seal killing in Namibia.

Sea lions, Scammon observed, "live upon fish, mollusks, crustaceans and sea-fowls; always with the addition of a few pebbles or smooth stones, some of which are a pound in weight." Many seals, in fact, occasionally swallow stones, but sea lions make a habit of it (as do crocodiles, which sometimes swallow masses of fist-sized stones). Sea lions swallow them and later vomit them.

I often watched this on the subantarctic Auckland Islands south of New Zealand, where I spent an austral summer with Hooker's sea lions. Typically, a young sea lion male

A Hooker's sea lion pup rests upon its mother's flipper in the Auckland Islands.

◄　　*A Hooker's sea lion mother with her newborn pup in the Auckland Islands.*

would appear extremely unhappy—he'd have that seasick look. He'd rear up on front flippers, head drooping, eyes half-shut, then would retch and burp. The spasms would become more frequent and violent, until, with one final convulsion, the agonized animal would spew out half a dozen stones. He'd shake his head, saliva flying, burp again and then, with a look of infinite relief, move aside, sigh deeply and go to sleep.

Sea lions regularly ingest stones on the sea bottom near shore, gulping anything from pebbles to rocks the size of golf balls. Scientists have found more than a hundred of these gastroliths in the stomach of one animal, and nearly twenty-five pounds of stones in the stomach of another.

Why? More than 200 years ago, the Swedish scientist Karl von Linné in his book *Systema naturae* said seals, "to avoid hunger pangs, swallow stones that fill their stomachs." Since then, many other theories have been advanced to explain the stone swallowing of sea lions: the rocks serve as ballast to make diving easier for fat, buoyant sea lions; most sea lions are infested with a multitude of internal parasites and the stones grind up these unwelcome tenants; the stones aid in the maceration of food, especially the tough, rubbery squid sea lions swallow whole (all seals gulp their food—they never chew; their sharp, strong teeth are designed for catching and holding, not chewing). There are plenty of conjectures but no certainty.

One thing, though, is certain. When hundreds of sea lions cough up thousands of stones over thousands of years, the result is an amazing mass of stones. On the Snares Islands between New Zealand and Antarctica lie strange deposits of smooth stones. The Snares are composed of granite, but the stones are basalt. This geological riddle was solved in the 1940s by the researcher C. A. Fleming, who published his findings in a

A young Hooker's sea lion in the Auckland Islands vomits gastroliths—ingested stones—together with food remains. Stones may help to macerate tough, rubbery squid.

journal of petrology. The stones, he explained, had traveled in the stomachs of Auckland Islands Hooker's sea lions, which had vomited them onto the Snares beaches. The article was entitled "Sea Lions as Geological Agents."

More than a century ago, Scammon predicted that the sea lions "on the California coast will soon be exterminated." That has not happened. California sea lions are, in fact, increasing, and now number about 150,000. The southern sea lion is slowly declining. The Australian sea lion, never numerous, is probably holding its own, as is the Hooker's, rarest of all sea lions, with a total population of only about 5,000. But the largest of all sea lions, the majestic Steller sea lion of the North, has suffered a catastrophic decline. In 1961, the total Steller sea lion population was thought to be between 240,000 and 300,000. Thirty years later, in 1991, only an estimated 40,000 were left.

When I observed Steller sea lions during one summer fifteen years ago on Marmot Island off Alaska, more than 10,000 sea lions crowded the seven rookeries, and each season about 5,000 pups were born. Now many beaches are empty; fewer than 3,000 sea lions were counted during a recent summer breeding season. Lack of food due to over-fishing by humans seems to be a major reason for this rapid decline.

It is fascinating, and sad, to read Chekhov's description of the marine wealth near Sakhalin Island a century ago, before the fleets of many nations, in fierce rivalry, despoiled this sea as they have despoiled most others. In late July and early August, Chekhov wrote, salmon ascended the rivers and "the surface of the river . . . seems to be

Like a sculpture in bronze, a young male Galápagos sea lion stands on shore ▶
in the late-evening sun.

seething. The water has a fishy taste, the oars are jammed, the blades propel the obstructing fish into the air."

Even more impressive was the spring herring run: "The approach of the herring can always be detected: a circular band of white foam covering a tremendous stretch of sea, flocks of gulls and albatrosses, whales spouting, herds of sea lions. The scene is magnificent! The number of whales following the herring is so great that [the explorer] Krusenstern's ship was encircled by them and it was only with extreme caution that they could reach the bank. During the herring run, the sea appears to be boiling over."

The California sea lion is the smallest of the world's five sea lion species. Although a bane, perhaps, to fishermen, the animals are a joy to all who love watching seals. I observed these sea lions and a few northern elephant seals from a cliff on Santa Barbara Island, one of California's Channel Islands. They seemed to exemplify extremes of seal behavior. The elephant seals, defeated and hence unemployed males, lay on the beach and slept. Between 8:00 a.m. and 4:30 p.m. when the tide covered the beach, they moved only five or six times—usually just to raise the head, stare vaguely in the distance with large, dark eyes, sigh deeply, so that the long trunk fluttered and bubbled, before they subsided and went to sleep again.

In the meantime, on wave-washed rocks the sea lions played with marvelous grace and abandon. Beautifully streamlined, they soared through the water. They jostled one another off the rocks, playing King of the Castle; jumped out of the water, backs arched; planed sideways through the front of a wave; rode its foamy crest until it looked as if they

◀ *On the Galápagos Islands, a yearling Galápagos sea lion pup climbs onto its mother's back.*

A cautious little swimmer. An Australian sea lion pup's first venture into the sea near Kangaroo Island, Australia.

must be shattered against the dark lava rocks; twisted around at the last moment; and, in a sparkling somersault, dove through the wave and emerged in deep, dark water beyond it.

That night I wrote in my diary: "God surely made these sea lions on the first day of Creation, when He was still full of pep and joy and inspiration; and on the sixth day, when He was very tired, He made the elephant seal—and man."

Outlined by the setting sun, California sea lions in late evening upon the beach of San Miguel Island. ▶

Gleaming Steller sea lions on a wave-washed rock by Marmot Island, Alaska.

◄   *Steller sea lions on rocks above a sparkling sea at Round Island, Alaska.*

Pups in Peril

ILLER WHALES AND GREAT WHITE SHARKS are certainly bad for baby and adult seals, but a major danger for sea lion pups, at least, comes from their killing adult kin. Infanticide, accidental or intentional, is an important cause of pup mortality.

The Hooker's sea lion is the rarest and most mild mannered of all sea lions (seal scientists refer to them fondly as "the gentle Hookers"). Most breed on the Auckland Islands, 300 miles (500 km) south of New Zealand. I observed them for several months on Enderby, the northernmost island of this group, where, during the austral summer, about 600 sea lions mass on the broad, half-mile (.3 km) long breeding beach.

The bulls I watched were not actively hostile to pups and never attacked them; for all they cared, the pups might have been lumps of sand on the beach. But in their jealousy-prodded charges, 800-pound (360 kg) bulls galumphed blithely across just-born twelve-pound (5 kg) pups or absent-mindedly sat on a pup and squashed it. While the females did their best to shield their youngsters, they were rarely fast enough or strong enough to deflect a charging bull.

The sand is soft, and the pups are amazingly resilient; most survive being steamrollered by the huge males. The greatest danger came when a bull would stop abruptly right on top of a pup. He'd just sit there, a massive hulk, totally oblivious to the tiny creature squirming beneath him. Most females tried frantically but ineffectually to free their pinned pups; if a small flipper protruded from beneath the bull, they pulled it, usually without success. They never bite the bulls, but the New Zealand sea mammal expert

You mustn't swim till
  you're six weeks old
Or your head will be sunk
  by your heels;
And summer gales and
  Killer Whales
Are bad for baby seals.
—SEAL MOTHER'S SONG, IN
  RUDYARD KIPLING'S "THE
  WHITE SEAL"

*When Hooker's sea lion bulls battle, the tiny pups, here in the Auckland Islands,
rush to get out of harm's way.*

*Intensely hostile to pups other than her own, this Steller sea lion female on
Marmot Island in Alaska tosses an alien pup.* ▶

Martin Cawthorn once watched a female use a shrewd stratagem to free her pup. She moved provocatively in front of the bull and presented herself for mounting. The bull moved instantly to the female, which then repelled him, nuzzled her freed pup and led it to safety.

The pups are precocious and learn quickly. Within three or four days of birth, they know this threat and flipper frantically out of the way when Big Daddy comes barging along. A few days later, they leave the crowded, dangerous rookery and settle in pup pods near its periphery.

There they are safe from death by trampling bulls, but they are often pestered by obnoxious juvenile males. These three- to five-year-old males are the restless ruffians of the beaches. They playfight with one another, but some also use pups as female substitutes: they herd them, try to form and keep pup "harems" and occasionally attempt to mate with squirming, protesting pups. However, they are not brutal, and when the pups are really fed up, they quickly escape.

The pups of southern sea lions are less fortunate. During a four-year study conducted at Peninsula Valdés in Argentina by Claudio Campagna of the University of California and his colleagues, immature male sea lions seized pups on 285 occasions. Some were individual kidnappings; others were raids carried out by several subadult males acting together. While adult male and female southern sea lions do not injure pups, the subadult males "appear to use pups as female substitutes to redirect their frustrated sexual and aggressive motivations," reported Campagna. During his study, 5.6 percent of the abducted pups died from injuries caused by subadult males.

In Steller sea lions it is the female that is more deadly than the male, and Steller sea

An Australian sea lion bull kills a cowering pup on Kangaroo Island, Australia.

lion pups face a rough initiation into the world. The moment a pup is born, its mother grabs it, raises it a few feet above the beach and drops it onto the rocks—the sea lion version of a slap upon a human baby's bottom. She repeats this (one scientist observed a female picking up and dropping her newborn pup fifty-two times in a row!) until the pup cries and crawls. Then the female sniffs her pup and listens intently to its voice; from that moment on, she can pick out her baby from all others on the beach.

Steller sea lion pups are tough little creatures and easily survive the postpartum pounding. But their ordeal is far from over. Steller sea lion cows are intensely maternal and protective with their own pups, and fiercely hostile to all other pups. During its first week of life, a pup does not recognize its mother's voice and may crawl hopefully toward any calling cow on the beach—a move that can be fatal. If a female upon sniffing the pup decides it is not hers, she snarls, grabs it and tosses it yards away. Landing in the private sphere of another cow, the poor pup may be grabbed and flung again, then thrown back and forth by hostile females, like a screaming, flippered rag doll.

Most dangerous to pups are the insanely jealous Australian sea lion bulls. In other sea lion species, top bulls have harems. Each high-ranking Australian sea lion male usually keeps only one female, and he will attack and try to kill anyone coming near her, including pups. Some females try to defend pups, their own or others, but it rarely helps. Bulls attack pups with concentrated lethal fury, biting and shaking them the way a terrier shakes a rat and leaving them crushed upon the beach.

A pup on Kangaroo Island in Australia fights for its life. The Australian sea lion bull attacks it in ▶
the shallows, but before the bull can kill the pup, it squirms free and escapes.

In this species, the mother, when she goes to sea to feed, hides her pup in a niche or crevice or beneath piled boulders where a bull cannot reach it. Even this precaution does not always protect pups from murderous males.

Near the cliff from which I watched the breeding beach on Kangaroo Island one summer, a female about to give birth had come ashore. Another female, now at sea, had hidden her three-week-old pup among a pile of boulders at the base of this cliff. Within a few hours of the pregnant female's arrival, a patrolling top bull had found her. He guarded her with possessive vigilance and fended off the attention of several encroaching males. Three days later, a young male tentatively crossed into the exclusive sphere of the resident bull and was instantly attacked. For one moment the rivals faced each other, then the young bull turned and fled. The huge bull, seething with unspent fighting spirit, his mouth wide open and vibrissae abristle, waddled back to his post.

At this moment, the long-hidden pup emerged from its refuge among the boulders. Probably hungry, it may have mistaken the pregnant female for its mother. When the bull saw the movement, he immediately lunged and grabbed the pup before it could flee. The pregnant female attacked and bit the bull, but to no avail. He shook the little pup, flung it ten feet (3 m), rushed after it, grabbed it anew, then shook and tossed it again. Each movement of the desperate youngster incited the bull to new attacks, until the pup lay dead. Eventually, the beach's resident Rosenberg's goanna, a nearly seven foot (2 m) long monitor lizard patrolling the area for carrion, found the mangled pup and ate it.

PRACTICE MAKES THE BEACHMASTER

TYPICALLY IN SEA LION SOCIETY—apart from the atypical Australian sea lion—there is a division of age groups. The breeding rookery is home to adult females, their newborn pups and the top bulls that control segments of the rookery and the females upon them. A few days after birth, pups leave the dangerous region, with those great bulls that trample little pups like juggernauts, and seek safety and mutual comfort in pup pods at the edge of the rookery.

Far from the rookery, on separate beaches, defeated bulls rest and recover. Some may try another battle, but most seem resigned to the fact that—this season, at least—the fighting, and the hope of winning territory and females, is over.

Near the rookery, but at a respectful distance from the master males, are small herds of bachelor bulls, three- to five-year-old immature males that aspire some day to be alpha bulls. In the meantime they all playfight, and the older ones try to sneak some sex on the sly.

About the size and color of adult females, these young males are active and feisty, venturesome yet fearful. Their playfights are highly ritualized, similar to the fights of adult males but less furious and never bloody; they may nip each other, but they do not bite.

Two young males face each other, growl and grunt like big bulls, hack at each other but do no damage as they rear up, chest against chest, heave and push, eyes bulging with exertion, and try to topple the adversary. They rest and pant, cool down, and then the next pushing match begins. Suddenly one "surrenders"—he throws himself down, flippers spread out on the sand. It is a submissive pose. Adult bulls use it, too, a sort of armistice between fighting bouts to avoid overheating.

A female Hooker's sea lion repels the advances of a massive male upon a beach of the subantarctic Auckland Islands.

The young males playfight endlessly with each other, or round up reluctant pups to practice "harem keeping." The Hooker's, which are the mildest of all sea lions, are rarely rough with the pups, and after a while, when the pups have had enough, they scatter, and the young males, which still have a lot to learn about keeping harems, do not know how to stop them.

Those are the games of the three- and four-year-old males. The five-year-olds already have more ambitious ideas. Far too young and light to face a massive adult bull and win territory and females, they try to insinuate themselves into the rookery and find a receptive female. It is a risky business (akin to a skinny teenage boy paying court to the lovely young wife of the world's greatest boxer) and these young males know it. The adventurous young males on the make have two advantages: a big bull with many wives is very busy and cannot be everywhere at once, and these young males look very much like females.

The greatest problem of these young hopefuls is that adult females rarely accept them. Having slipped with infinite caution into the rookery, keeping, literally, a very low profile, a young male tries a few tentative courting nibbles at the neck and chest of a female. Far from being pleased, she nearly always loudly and angrily rebuffs him. Alerted by the noise, the resident bull charges, and the young swain flees. If he is cornered by an adult bull, he usually assumes the submission posture of a female. This seems to confuse the big bull, and while he hesitates, the young lothario escapes unscathed.

In Steller sea lions this "game" is more complicated. An entire bevy of young males may rush ashore together, gallop helter-skelter over the densely packed and loudly protesting females, then try to lie low among them to avoid detection or rush right to the land side of the rookery. From time to time the territorial male, a fearsome one-ton bull with great power and long, yellow canines, routs these trespassers. Often he spots only one of them, and if the others would just stay put and lie low, he would probably not notice them because they look so much like females. But they seem possessed of a common guilty conscience mingled with fear, and the moment one flees, all flee, and there is pandemonium in the rookery as those frantic young males race across the massed females to the saving sea.

If such a young male is cornered by a furious territorial bull, he instantly starts a complex but effective appeasement ritual: he shakes his head rapidly from side to side, mouth wide open, jaw slack, yammers and tries to nibble the neck of the dominant male (this is precisely the gesture of a female in estrus!). This inhibits the territorial bull from annihilating the interloper, and while the great lord dithers, the youngster, still yammering, backs away, turns suddenly and rushes off to safety.

Thus, slowly, year by year, the males gain strength and fighting skills until, at about the age of seven, they have the weight and power to compete with other adult bulls for territory. They may start modestly, with a small territory at the edge of the rookery and a female or two, and advance, if they have the power, in a couple of years to top bull on prime territory that is covered with females. A top bull rarely holds that exalted position for more than two or three years. The strain is immense, and the competition fierce. In sea lions, fur seals and elephant seals the descent from alpha bull to omega and utter defeat is rapid and nearly always final.

*A young male Hooker's sea lion in the Auckland Islands has rounded up pups to practice
"harem keeping." Exhausted from the effort, he sleeps, and the pups will scatter.*

California sea lion males challenge each other on a San Miguel Island beach.

Flexible and furious, young southern elephant seals have mock battles on a Falkland Islands beach.

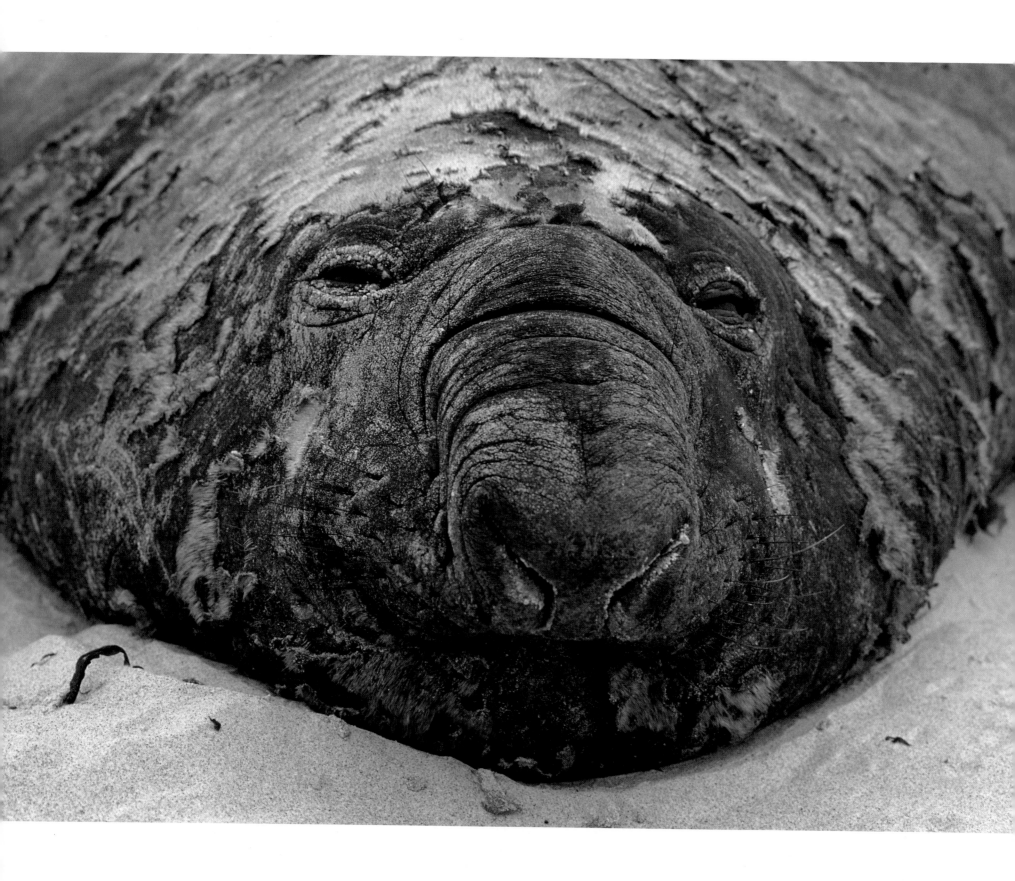

PART III

EARLESS SEALS

◀ *Largest of all pinnipeds, the southern elephant seal weighs up to 8,000 pounds*
(3,600 kg). Here, a male rests on the Falkland Islands.

TRUE SEALS

O MOST ENGLISH-SPEAKING PEOPLE a seal is simply a seal; to the French it is a *phoque*; to Germans *Seehund* (sea dog) or *Robbe*; to Spaniards *foca* or *becerro marino* (sea calf); and French-Canadians call it *loup marin* (sea wolf).

Taxonomists, to whom simplicity is anathema, term all seals "pinnipeds" and divide them into three families with a total of thirty-three species. First there are the eared seals, or Otariidae (from the Greek *otarion*—"little ear"); they include the sea lions and fur seals, which have neat, furry little ears. Then come the earless seals, or Phocidae, which have no external ears. Finally there are the Odobenidae (meaning "tooth walkers" in Greek), with the long-tusked walrus the only member of this family. Just to complicate matters, earless seals are also called "true seals," which seems like a sneer at all other seals (but is still mild compared with what taxonomists call each other!).

Reflecting their different ancestry, eared and earless seals are different in appearance, movement and behavior.

Eared seals, the fur seals and sea lions, are agile on land and swim with their front flippers in the sea. Earless seals, or Phocids, are slow on land and swim by sculling with their broad hind flippers.

The breeding strategy of the two families is totally different, too. Eared seals gather annually at ancestral rookeries. Males conquer and hold territories. Females haul out onto these territories, bear pups a day or two after arriving, mate soon after and then go periodically to sea to feed. They nurse their pups from a few months to a year or more, depending on the species. Phocid females haul out thickly padded with blubber and transfer that fat, via extremely fat-rich milk, to their pups. Many do not feed at all during the

A bearded seal rests on water-seamed summer ice near Ellesmere Island in Canada's High Arctic.

lactation period. They stay with their pups until they are weaned, about eight weeks in the ringed seal and only four days in the hooded seal.

Earless seals do not live in dense rookeries. They have favorite islands where they breed and haul out to rest or molt, but they do not form dense breeding groups dominated by powerful males that hold territories. Some, like the gray seals, are gregarious and lie close together on their breeding islands—Sable Island in the Atlantic off eastern Canada, for example, or North Rona off Scotland (*rona* means "seal" in Gaelic). Others, such as the bearded seal of the Arctic, are solitary. They meet and mate and swim their separate ways. Females bear their pups on ice floes, far from one another.

Whereas eared seals—the fur seals and sea lions—are dramatically dimorphic, with some massive males five times heavier than their females, phocids exhibit no great size difference between the sexes. The males of gray and hooded seals are larger than the females; in harbor, ringed and harp seals, males and females are roughly the same size, weight and color; and in monk and Weddell seals females are usually larger than the males. (Two earless seals do not conform: the giant elephant seals of the North and of the South. In these two species, the male is much larger than the female; males and females congregate annually at ancestral rookeries; males have spectacular fights with one another and winners hold territories and mate, as a rule, with the females upon their territories. In short, they behave very much like fur seals and sea lions, but they have no external ears and are consequently members of the earless seal family.)

Two of the earless seals live in landlocked bodies of water: the Caspian seal in the Caspian Sea and the Baikal seal in Siberia's Lake Baikal.

Two species of earless seals live in warm climates: the Mediterranean and the

Short flippers and a fat body make it difficult for molting harbor seals on Sable Island, Canada, to reach itchy places.

Its downy natal coat crusted with snow, a gray seal pup sleeps after a snowstorm on Sable Island, Canada.

A small ringed seal surfaces in the Arctic sea. Circumpolar and numerous,
it is the polar bear's principal prey.

Hawaiian monk seals, and so did their recently extinct cousin (last seen in 1952), the Caribbean monk seal.

Eleven Phocid species are pagophilic—they love ice. The ringed, Caspian, Baikal, harp, ribbon, hooded and bearded seals of the North, and the Weddell, Ross, crabeater and leopard seals of the Far South breed, as a rule, exclusively on ice. In an iceless year, harp seals will abort at sea rather than pup on land. Harp seals make great annual migrations, whereas harbor, gray, bearded and ringed seals rarely leave their home range.

The family of earless seals includes the largest of all pinnipeds, the colossal southern elephant seal—a male can be more than sixteen feet (5 m) long and weigh 8,000 pounds (3600 kg)—and the smallest of all pinnipeds, the diminutive Baikal seal—just over three feet (1 m) long, it weighs about 150 pounds (68 kg).

The Phocids are a varied, widespread family. They include the little known, yet most numerous of all seals, the crabeater (population thirty million and increasing), which lives in the hard-to-reach antarctic pack ice; and the longest studied (since Aristotle, for more than 2,000 years), the Mediterranean monk seal. Its image already graced Greek coins in 500 B.C.; it had towns named after it, such as Foça in Turkey (once the great Ioanian city of Phocaea); and an entire region of ancient Greece was known as Phocis. Today, with only about 500 left, it hovers on the brink of extinction.

◄ *At the beginning of their midwinter breeding season, gray seals haul ashore on Sable Island in the Atlantic.*

Some Phocids, such as the monk seals, are strictly protected. Others, such as the harp seal, are still intensively hunted and have been killed in the millions for more than 200 years. The harp seal hunt was, as the American author George Allan England said in his 1924 book, "the greatest hunt in the world," and it is still the largest and most controversial seal hunt today.

Fast and lethal, the leopard seal of the Antarctic regions is a powerful predator.
It eats penguins and seal pups, but also fish.

LIFE AND DEATH ON THE ICE

IN MARCH 1964, I took a picture of a pure-white harp seal pup on the Front Ice off northern Newfoundland. The pup looked at me with large, dark, appealing eyes; somehow light, mood and composition were perfect. The pup was innocence incarnate and the photograph captured this.

The picture gained considerable fame. It became an early emblem of the environmental movement. It appeared on myriad posters and placards with the opening line from the refrain of the Beatles' song "Let It Be." In 1989, this picture was among fifty-one chosen for the book *Photographs That Changed the World*.

In March 1997, I was again on the ice with the harp seals. It was my twenty-seventh season with these seals, my annual pilgrimage to a very beautiful and special world, the immense nursery of harp seals upon the pack ice in Canada's Gulf of St. Lawrence, a place of birth and also of death.

I wandered across the ice. Seals, like humans, are individualistic. Some females are fearful, some aggressive, and the odd one is friendly. I found a friendly female and lay down on the ice close to her. Her newborn pup, its downy fur still tinted yellowish by amniotic fluid, slept nearby. When it awoke, hungry (the normal state of harp seal pups, which must double or triple their birth weight in the two weeks before their mothers leave them), it crawled to the nearest dark shape—me. It was all innocence, too young to know my alien smell, and butted me urgently in the side, a signal that it wanted to nurse.

It has not been easy to convey to the Eskimo mind the meaning of the Oriental similies of the Bible. Thus the Lamb of God had to be translated kotik or young seal. This animal, with its perfect whiteness as it lies in its cradle of ice, its gentle, helpless nature, and its pathetic innocent eyes, is probably as apt a substitute, however, as nature offers.
—DR. WILFRED T. GRENFELL, MEDICAL MISSIONARY TO LABRADOR, 1909

Having molted its white natal coat, the young harp seal, now called a "beater," is alone on the ice. ▶
Its mother has long since left.

I turned it gently and pushed it toward its mother, only seven feet (2 m) away. Soon the pup was eagerly drinking its mother's warm, fat-rich milk, eyes closed in utter bliss. Finally full, the pup rolled onto its back and played with its flippers, idly curious and deeply content. Mother and pup were totally oblivious to my presence, and I enjoyed my little corner of paradise upon the ice in the spring sun.

Not far away, sealers were killing the pups. As we flew back to Prince Edward Island in the evening, great areas of ice beneath us were blotched and streaked in red where seal pups had been clubbed to death, skinned and their sculps (pelts plus blubber) hauled to central pans from which hired helicopters slung load after load of blood-dripping pelts to shore. Dark spots dotted the ice—the flayed corpses of the little pups. We did not land. It would have been illegal. "Observers and writers are not wanted by the seal hunters," wrote the American George Allan England in 1924 in the best book written about the seal hunt, *Vikings of the Ice*, later reprinted as *The Greatest Hunt in the World*.

The harp seal is a seal of the ice; its early scientific name was *Pagophilus*—"the ice lover." Its whole life cycle and vast annual migrations move in rhythm with the formation and disintegration of the vast northern ice fields. After pupping, mating and molting in March and April, the great Canadian harp seal herds swim toward western Greenland. They reach it in June and scatter along the food-rich, fjord-serrated coast as far north as the Thule district.

As the far-northern ice breaks up in July and August, some of the seals move west into the straits and bays of the Canadian Arctic archipelago, some remain near Greenland's coast, and some swim into Hudson Bay. Thus, although their numbers are immense (in prehunting times, perhaps ten million; now, about three million), the seals

Her whiskers pearled with ice, a harp seal mother looks at her pup on the ice of Canada's
Gulf of St. Lawrence.

Four hours old, a brand-new harp seal pup plays with its flipper near its mother on the Gulf of St. Lawrence ice.

are scattered over a sea area of more than a million square miles (2.5 million sq. km), and competition for food is relatively slight in any one region.

Harp seals are pelagic; they haul out onto ice to breed and molt but spend the rest of the year at sea. They do not haul out on the ice floes of the Far North, thus avoiding their most dangerous enemy—after man—the polar bear. They swim in groups. I have flown many seal surveys in the Arctic: the solitary ringed and bearded seals are hard to spot and count. The gregarious harp seals can't be missed. They swim in happy pods of from twenty to sixty animals, dive together, maybe hunt together, and then surface in a swirl of joyous abandon: *kairulit*, the Inuit call them, "the jumping seals."

In September, as ice begins to form in the far North, the seals begin the southward part of their annual 6,200 miles (10,000 km) migration to return in March to the breeding ice that used to be so wonderfully safe because it was south of the polar bear's normal range.

There are three distinct and discrete harp seal populations, or herds, known by the location of their breeding ice: the first, the Newfoundland herd, is split into the Front herd, which breeds on the pack ice off Newfoundland and Labrador, and the Gulf herd, which breeds on the ice in the Gulf of St. Lawrence, the "most southerly part of the Northern Hemisphere to be covered by winter sea ice," according to a scientific report.

The West Ice herd breeds on the pack ice east of Greenland, and the White Sea herd breeds on the ice of Russia's White Sea.

Fishermen in Canada, both French and English, killed some harp seals (as well as harbor and gray seals) in the seventeenth and eighteenth centuries, but the great commercial hunt began about 1800 and soared to a peak in 1831, when sealing ships returned with 680,000 pelts. During the entire nineteenth century, the average annual kill was about 350,000; in the twentieth century it has been about 200,000. In 1934, a Newfoundland sealing captain, Abram Kean, brought in his one-millionth seal, which earned him the Order of the British Empire!

Since 1800, sealers and whalers (seal hunting was a profitable sideline for them; in 1889, for example, whalers killed 300,000 seals on the Front) took more than fifty million harp seals. Millions of molting seals were shot and lost; according to Captain Kean, nineteen seals were shot and lost for each one shot and retrieved. Millions of piled pelts were lost on wind-dispersed floes. About 500 sealing ships sank with their sealskin cargoes (and more than a thousand sealers died, 255 in 1914 alone). If you add to all this the harp seals killed on the ice east of Greenland and in Russia's White Sea, you arrive at the amazing, and sad, total of more than seventy million harp seals killed in the past 200 years.

The hunt continues. The official Canadian kill quota was raised from 186,000 in 1995, to 250,000 in 1996, to 275,000 in 1997, and large numbers of harp seals are still killed on the ice of Russia's White Sea. The main incentive now, in addition to pelts, is the sale of seal penises to China. The harp seal hunt was—and is—the greatest, most protracted mass slaughter ever inflicted upon any wild mammal species.

A harp seal pup leans far forward to "kiss" its surfacing mother. Mutual identification is mainly by smell.

*A sealer has killed and skinned a harp seal pup and now hauls the pelt plus blubber
to a central pan from which helicopters sling the pelts ashore.*

◄ *A young Italian tourist hugs a harp seal pup.*

SEALS OF THE HOLY SEA

T IS CALLED "THE PEARL OF SIBERIA," Lake Baikal, "the Holy Sea."
As God created Siberia, an ancient legend tells, he accidental-
ly dropped his most precious pearl and it turned into a deep
blue lake of supernatural beauty. The most popular folk song in
Siberia (originally a convict song) about this vast lake in the
very heart of Asia, begins, "The sacred Baikal, the glorious Sea."

Filling a deep rift in the earth, Lake Baikal is 400 miles
(650 km) long and 50 miles (80 km) wide at its widest, and stunningly beautiful in its
many moods. Lead gray in stormy weather, a rippled green in a wooded cove, Lake Baikal
is a deep sapphire blue on sunny days, its oxygen-rich, pellucid water so crystal clear you
can see pebbles on the lake bottom at a depth of 130 feet (40 m).

It is a lake of superlatives: It is twenty-five million years old, the most ancient lake
on earth. It is 5,370 feet (1,637 m) deep, more than a mile, the deepest lake on earth. It
holds one-fifth of the earth's fresh water, more water than North America's five Great
Lakes combined.

Bai-kul means "rich lake" in Buryat, the language of the Mongol people who live
around the lake (today, along with people from many regions of Russia). More than
2,000 species of animals and plants inhabit this ancient lake and about 80 percent of them
are endemic: native to Lake Baikal and nowhere else in the world. Most famous is the
Baikal seal (*Phoca sibirica*), smallest of all seals, locally known as *nerpa*, which lives in this
freshwater lake 1,996 miles (3,220 km) from the nearest ocean.

It is not the world's only freshwater seal. Long ago ringed seals with wanderlust
ascended the Neva River and now live in Lake Ladoga, north of St. Petersburg. Lake

*The Tartars call it the Holy
Sea ... [and] it produces
great numbers of seals.*
—JOHN BELL, SCOTTISH
PHYSICIAN TO THE RUSSIAN
DELEGATION TRAVELING
OVERLAND FROM
ST. PETERSBURG TO PEKING,
1720–1722

Saimaa, in Finland, also has a resident seal population. Both *Phoca hispida saimensis* and *Phoca hispida ladogensis* are considered subspecies of the ringed seal. Seals descended from harbor seals of Hudson Bay live in the landlocked Upper and Lower Seal Lakes in Ungava, in arctic Quebec. And when I traveled years ago with Indian hunters up the Seal River in northern Manitoba, we came to Seal Lake, another home of freshwater harbor seals.

The Baikal seal, a close relative of the circumpolar arctic ringed seal, has been in the lake for about 13,000 years (much longer, some scientists claim), after reaching it by flood-swollen rivers during the Pleistocene. The seals are tubby, but have a gorgeous silver-gray fur. Today about 70,000 of them live in Lake Baikal. The Buryats, wrote Dr. Bell in 1720, catch the seals with "strong nets hung under the ice." Both the meat and blubber were eaten—the blubber was considered a great delicacy—and the skins were used for clothing. Seal oil from Lake Baikal, from remotest times, was carried by camel caravans to Tibet, to burn in the oil lamps of the monks.

In March, like ringed seals, female Baikal seals excavate snow lairs upon the ice and in these igloos (called *nunarjaks* by the Inuit of the Arctic) bear their tiny, seven-pound (3 kg) pups, which are wrapped in long, downy soft, white natal fur.

The seal's favorite food is the *golomyanka*, an endemic oilfish of Lake Baikal and the strangest of the lake's fifty-two fish species. It is a small fish, only six to eight inches (15 to 20 cm) long, it has no swim bladder or scales, it is pale pink and looks like frosted glass, and is so transparent you can nearly read newsprint through it. And if you hold it

Evening mists roll over Lake Baikal, the world's oldest and deepest lake and home to the world's smallest seal, the Baikal seal. ▶

in your hand on a warm, sunny day, it simply melt away, because 35 percent of its body weight consists of a fine oil that is extremely rich in vitamin A.

The *golomyanka* are the most numerous fish in Lake Baikal, yet they are not commercially fished because they never shoal. They migrate vertically. Feeding on amphipods, they rise to the lake surface at night and descend to the abyss in daytime. The seals hunt the *golomyanka* at night and eat such masses of these oily fish that it is little wonder they are so fat.

I had read a lot about Lake Baikal and its seals, and the main reason my wife and I traveled by train to Irkutsk in Siberia was to visit nearby Lake Baikal and, we hoped, see its seals.

But it was the Brezhnev era; travel for foreigners in the then Soviet Union was extremely restricted and the standard answer to all requests was *Nyet!* ("No!") or *Nye moshno!* ("It is impossible!"). I think bureaucrats got prizes for being obnoxious and unhelpful.

And yet, every once in a while, like a lovely ray of sunshine, the real Russian soul, with its spontaneous kindness and generosity, would break through this gloomy gray cloud of bureaucratic boorishness.

Scientists at Lake Baikal, obviously carefully briefed, were helpful enough as long as I wanted scientific information. They deluged me with data, statistics and set speeches about the glorious achievements of Communism. But the moment I asked for help to see the seals, it was "impossible." No boat, no seals, no hope. Not now. Not ever.

Small and curious, a Baikal seal swims slowly close to shore at a tree-girt bay of Lake Baikal. ▶

While they parried all my requests, I noticed one young scientist speaking quietly to our KGB escort and making drawings on paper. After the obligatory drinks, toasts and expressions of mutual goodwill, we left. At the car the KGB escort, a youngish man with red hair, stopped and said, "Fred Aristovich, listen. I know you came here to see seals. A scientist told me there is a bay not very far from here where the seals often come close to shore. I will take you there. But do not tell it to anyone. You understand, this is dangerous for me."

We drove, then walked to the sheltered bay. "Your wife and I," he said, "will go and eat and drink tea and talk [he spoke fluent French]. We'll pick you up in the evening. Don't go anywhere else and don't speak to anyone. Good luck!"

I hid behind some rocks, set up tripod and camera and waited. The taiga surrounding the lake glowed with the colors of fall: gold and silver birches, amber-yellow soaring larches and gnarled, dark pines anchored to the rocks.

Suddenly a round little head appeared in the shimmering water—a seal surfacing far away. I wanted to draw it closer and used a tactic that works with ringed seals. These arctic animals, especially when young, have one trait that Inuit exploit to lure them into shooting range: they are terribly curious. On the assumption that the Baikal seal might share this characteristic, I tried all the wiles I had learned from Inuit friends: I whistled, I mewed, I made the most peculiar noises.

Consumed with curiosity, the little seal approached. I caterwauled and it drew closer, a little brown head with large, dark eyes, straw-colored whiskers and four stiff white hairs above each eye, sculling gently with its hind flippers, curious, desperately curious, about all those strange noises. It swam slowly to within a few yards of me, but then a second, more seasoned seal appeared, came close, noticed a movement and dove with a splash, and my curious, careless little friend fled, too.

In the evening the KGB man returned. "Did you see the *nerpa?*" he asked. "Yes!" I answered. He smiled. "Then I am happy," he said, and drove us back to our hotel in Irkutsk.

Seals of Beaches and Bays

HOOVER, THE TALKING HARBOR SEAL, lived at the New England Aquarium in Boston (hence the Boston accent) and didn't say much until he was seven years old. Then he began to imitate human words and phrases. He could say "Hoover," "Hello," "Come over here" and "Get out of there," and he laughed a lot—"heh, heh, heh." He slurred his words, but, as England's famous sage and wit Dr. Samuel Johnson said in 1763 in another context (apropos of women preaching), "It is not done well: but you are surprised to find it done at all."

That a harbor seal should "talk" is, of course, surprising. But these seals are on familiar, though normally distant, terms with humans. While other seals, rightly, shun the vicinity of humans, harbor seals do not seek it, but humans have encroached upon what long ago was the seals' private property: the bays, beaches and estuaries of northern Europe and much of North America. Hence their name: harbor, or common, seal.

For most people in Europe and North America who have seen a seal "in the wild," this is the seal: it is that round, bewhiskered head you see bobbing far out in the bay; it is the seal that trails your boat, usually at a cautious distance; it is the seal you see basking on sandbanks and on offshore rocks. Until most harbor seals were killed by a viral disease in 1988 that caused the death of at least 20,000 of them in Europe, about 7,000 lazed away their idle hours on The Wash, a famous beach and sandbar area sixty miles (100 km) north of London.

Unlike the pelagic harp or hooded seals, which haul out on ice only to breed and

[The captive male harbor seal named Hoover] sounds like a male human with a Boston accent. He often sounds somewhat inebriated, probably because of his tendency to slur together sounds representing separate human words.

—DR. KATHERINE RALLS, ET AL. "VOCALIZATION AND VOCAL MIMICRY IN CAPTIVE HARBOR SEALS, *PHOCA VITULINA*," *CANADIAN JOURNAL OF ZOOLOGY*, 1985

Sculling with its hind flippers, a curious harbor seal rises high out of the water for a good look around.

molt, and spend the rest of their lives at sea, harbor seals like land: they feed at sea, then rest and sleep onshore, alone or often in small groups, and in a few places in very large groups.

They are the seals of our shores and (including subspecies) their range is immense: northern Europe from France to the north tip of Norway; the coasts of southern Greenland; the coasts of Atlantic North America from northern Baffin Island to North Carolina; and on the Pacific side, in the immense arc of the North Pacific from Baja California up to Alaska, out to the Aleutian Islands, across to the Kurile Islands and down to Japan.

Unlike so many far-roving seal species, harbor seals are homebodies. They live their entire lives along a relatively small home range of familiar coastline. Yet some do wander. They like estuaries and from there, in pursuit of prey, they swim upriver. Most return. Some settle. And a few venture farther. In Canada they are common in the Maritimes and in the Gulf of St. Lawrence. They also live permanently on shores and islands in the lower St. Lawrence River. A few travel to Quebec City and the odd one swims all the way up the St. Lawrence River to Montreal, more than 600 miles (1,000 km) from the sea, and gets his picture into all the papers.

It is these riverine harbor seals that end up in lakes and, if they like them, settle there and become freshwater seals, and if the lakes are large enough, the seals will in time—say, a few million years—become a separate species, like the Baikal seal.

The "kiss of recognition." A harbor seal mother on Sable Island, Canada, identifies her pup by its smell. ▶

(OVERLEAF) Harbor seals laze on the beach of Tugidak, a remote island in the North Pacific, off Alaska.

Harbor seals, generally, are cautious and shy. Until a few years ago, they could be hunted legally in most of northern Europe. They are hunted in Canada but in the United States are protected by the Marine Mammal Protection Act of 1972. Still, in many areas hostile fishermen and local louts take potshots at them and harbor seals tend to be wary of humans.

In areas where they are truly safe and see harmless humans regularly, harbor seals can become quite trusting. They like to sleep on offshore rocks in Canada's Forillon National Park at the tip of Gaspé Peninsula in Quebec. About 200,000 tourists visit this park each year. Many stand on the beach and ooh and aah about the seals, take pictures, clap hands and shout, and the seals do not even bother to look up.

It is the same at Cambria in California, where I lived for a while. Just across from hotels, restaurants and inns is Moonstone Drive and its extensive beach, popular with tourists and with harbor seals. The seals, the same group every day, lie at low tide on rocks near shore, rest and worry little about people. They do have a precautionary sleep-wake rhythm: about every minute or so, one seal wakes up, looks around, arches and flexes its fat-cigar body, yawns, twists a bit and goes back to sleep, safe, indolent and content.

For most baby seals, being born is no joy; there is distinct postpartum trauma. A harp seal baby, for instance, lies cozy and safe in its mother's womb, the temperature a steady 98.6°F (37.8°C). And suddenly, with one powerful contraction, it is expelled into a hostile, frigid world: it can be -4°F (-20°C) and blowing; the moist pup shivers violently and looks pathetically unhappy. Steller sea lion mothers, as we have seen, drop their just-born pups onto rocks until they cry (they cry quickly!) to imprint their baby's voice.

And newborn sea lion pups can get steamrollered by giant monomaniacal males in pursuit of rivals.

But all seal pups, except for those of the harbor seal, remain on land or ice for weeks or even months after birth, and show curiosity but also fear when they first come near water. Of all pinniped pups, harbor seal pups are the only ones that must swim hours after birth. The female may give birth at low tide on a sandbar that is flooded at high tide. So there is little time. The pup is born, the female sniffs it eagerly and listens to its voice so she will know her pup from all other pups in the area, she nurses her little pup, the water rises and the pup, only hours old, must swim with its mother. It is a struggle. The pup is weak. Its flippers, tightly curled in the womb like petals of a closed rose, have never been flexed, and they flutter feebly from side to side. The pup holds its head high out of the water and sculls pathetically near its mother. If waves are high, it may ride on its mother's back. If there is danger, she may enfold the little pup with her front flippers and dive.

Despite such care, a pup is occasionally separated from its mother, often by yahoos who think it's fun to chase seals with fast motorboats, and unless she finds the pup, it will die. It lies on a beach or sandbar and cries loudly and woefully to attract its mother. These crying waifs, called *Heuler* (howlers) in German, are collected by a small army of dedicated volunteers in the Netherlands and in Germany, then reared at several special institutions with lots of love, thick cream and, later, herrings, and in September, when they weigh about eighty or ninety pounds (36 or 40 kg), they are released into areas where other harbor seals live.

There is one island in the world where harbor seals congregate in great numbers—

17,000 by one count many years ago. This is Tugidak in the far-northern reaches of the Pacific, southwest of Kodiak Island off Alaska. The seventeen-mile (28-km) long island is treeless, swampy, storm haunted and uninhabited. A chartered plane dropped me and my supplies off, the pilot promised to return in a few weeks, the plane roared off and I was alone on the lush green island, with thousands of seals, thousands of birds (including bald eagles, which on this treeless island nest on the ground) and what seemed like billions of mosquitoes. I lived in a tiny but sturdy hut built long ago by other seal researchers.

Although the island seems flat, it rises gradually toward the north, then ends abruptly in an earth cliff about a hundred feet (30 m) high. On a beach beneath this cliff, not far from my hut, more than a thousand harbor seals lolled upon the sand like contented blimps.

Despite the isolation of the island, the seals were wary. Most slept, but a few watched. Anything could frighten them—a passing eagle, the flutter of an alighting gull, even the faint drone of a large jet airliner flying more than 30,000 feet (10,000 m) overhead. As soon as the sentinels fled, all seals awoke and lolloped frantically toward the sea, adults first, followed by worried, bewildered pups. Once they were safe in the water, hundreds of bewhiskered heads bobbed up to see what the latest alarm had been all about. Satisfied, after a while, that there was no danger, they laboriously hauled out onto the beach again. Pups called, were sniffed and recognized, bonds were reestablished, and the seal herd went back to sleep.

◀ *A happy harbor seal pup on Sable Island in the Atlantic.*

After a few days I began to recognize certain animals. Harbor seals have lovely dappled coats. Patterns vary considerably and it was fairly easy to pick out individuals with distinct designs. An exceedingly fat male was plagued by persistent itches. He tried to scratch his back, but he was much too fat and his flippers far too short. He turned onto his back, head and flippers held high, and twisted and rubbed in the gritty sand with an "Oh, does that feel good" look on his face.

It was lovely to be alone on the island. On good days I watched "my" seals and took notes and pictures. On bad days I walked and watched birds. And on horrid days, I lay on the bunk of my snug little cabin, listened to the eldritch screeching of the storm and read book after book with that lovely total leisure of someone who has nothing else to do.

I never returned to Tugidak, but all the news I hear about it from scientist friends in Alaska is bad. The pinnipeds of the northernmost Pacific are declining, some, such as the northern fur seals, slowly, others, such as the Steller sea lions, with catastrophic rapidity. Harbor seals still come to Tugidak Island. They came in the thousands when I lived there. Now only a few hundred are left. Overfishing by humans is the most probable cause of their decline.

The Blessings of Blubber

(or, How To Grow Immensely Fat in Only Four Days)

EA ICE IS UNSTABLE: it can melt, break up or drift away. Most seals that breed on unstable ice, such as the bearded, harp and hooded seals, are therefore in a hurry during the vital and vulnerable period between the pups' birth and their independence from maternal care. Their survival trick is rapid energy transfer from mother to pup.

Essentially, these seals store surplus food energy upon their bodies as a thick, calorie-rich blubber layer. The mother converts this blubber into extremely fat-rich milk; the baby drinks it and reconverts it into blubber that serves both as insulation against cold and an energy reserve for the day when the fount of maternal milk ceases to flow. For most seal pups born on ice, life begins with a brief feast followed by a prolonged fast.

Harp seal pups are wrapped in dense, pure-white natal wool and weigh about twenty pounds (9 kg) at birth. The mother seals often lie near one another on the ice, but each one has a small private sphere that no other female may transgress. The newborn harp seal pup suckles frequently its mother's creamy, thick milk, which contains about 50 percent fat. The young seal gains four to five pounds (2 to 2.5 kg) each day until, at the end of the two-week nursing period, it has tripled or quadrupled its birth weight and more than doubled its girth. A few of the pups gain eighty pounds (36 kg) from birth to weaning and are so obese that their short flippers barely reach the ice.

Because in seal society fat is fortune, these are the pups most likely to survive and prosper. After weaning, the pups molt their natal wool, lie on the ice living off their fat reserves for about a month and then begin the long northward migration to the High Arctic seas, which are ice-free in summer.

The great hooded seal of the North breeds on pack ice not far from where the harp

Hooded seals breed on pack ice in late March. An excited male extrudes and inflates his nasal septum.

seals breed, but usually later, in the last two weeks of March. Like the harp seal, it hauls out onto ice only to breed and molt. And it, too, breeds south of the polar bear's present range. These similarities between harp and hooded seals gave rise to the assumption, long held, that hooded seal pups are nursed for two weeks or longer.

But hooded seals achieve the ultimate in high-speed nurture: four days from birth to weaning.

This amazing fact was discovered only recently by W. Don Bowen of Canada's Department of Fisheries and Oceans, Bedford Institute of Oceanography, and Olav T. Oftedal and Daryl J. Boness of the National Zoological Park of the Smithsonian Institution in Washington, D.C. Hooded seal milk, they found, has the color and consistency of rich, peach-tinted cream. It is the richest milk known: it contains the most dry matter (70 percent), fat (61 percent) and gross energy (5.9 kcal/g) reported for any mammalian milk.

A hooded seal pup drinks seventeen to twenty pounds (8 to 9 kg) of this superrich milk daily and gains about fifteen pounds (7 kg) each day, and in about four days it's all done. The pup is weaned and on its own. It is the shortest lactation period known for any mammal.

That this discovery comes so late is not surprising because the hooded seal is among the least known of all pinnipeds. A major breeding population, about 65,000 adult hooded seals, lives in Davis Strait, between Baffin Island and Greenland, and was known to nineteenth-century whalers. Rediscovered only in the 1970s, these Davis Strait seals breed on shifting, drifting floes in an area nearly the size of Great Britain and more than 185 miles (300 km) from the nearest land.

The hooded seal's other breeding areas are equally hostile, mobile and inaccessible: the Front Ice off Newfoundland and Labrador and the West Ice east of Greenland. A small population breeds on the usually more stable ice in the Gulf of St. Lawrence. The total population of hooded seals is about 500,000.

Both male and female hooded seals have smoky blue-gray coats, dappled with irregular black blobs and blotches. Males are nearly ten feet (3 m) long and weigh about 650 pounds (293 kg). Females are about eight feet (2.5 m) long, weigh an average of 350 pounds (158 kg) and balloon to 400 pounds (180 kg) and more prior to giving birth.

Hooded seals—or "hoods," as sealers call them—were formerly known as crested or bladder-nosed seals owing to their most distinctive features. When angered or provoked, the male inflates the flaccid black skin sac atop its head into a two-humped "hood." In an even more impressive display, to woo a female or threaten a rival, the male extrudes and inflates his nasal septum into an orange-red, soccer-ball-sized balloon, shakes it violently and deflates it with a loud gurgly-squishy pulsing sound.

Unlike the smaller, shyer harp seals, which usually flee when humans approach, large hooded seals often attack and can move with rapid undulations across the ice. "Sealers tell many fearsome tales of men losing leg or arm by dog-hood bites," wrote George Allan England in 1924.

Every year, there is a spattering of hooded seals upon the Gulf of St. Lawrence ice between Prince Edward Island and the Magdalen Islands. I usually spot the first ones about March 7 or 8. Prevailing winds and currents push the ice, and the hooded seals, toward the east, and in most years they vanish. In 1997, strong winds pushed the hooded seals' whelping ice against Cape Breton Island. There the ice got stuck, and it was a

The hooded seal owes its name to the skin sac atop the male's head that it inflates into a "hood."

Two hooded seal pups shortly after birth.

Passionately protective of her newborn pup, a sharp-toothed hooded seal mother attacks.

marvelous opportunity to visit the same seals regularly and watch what happens to seal pups that each day drink twenty pounds (9 kg) of the richest milk known.

On the first day, Telford Allen, longtime pilot of the International Fund for Animal Welfare (IFAW) and I flew high above the ice. Hooded seals are easy to spot: they usually lie in twos, a female and her pup, or in threes, female and pup, plus a male in waiting that would like to be the father of next year's pup.

Several groups lay not far from a lead, a stretch of open water. One female, near a distinctive, triangular ice block, had just given birth. Her pup had completed its first molt already in utero, shedding its light-gray embryonal coat. These hairs now lay like little felted grayish disks upon the ice together with the afterbirth.

The female became furious as I approached. Female hooded seals with newborn pups are passionately protective. She snarled and attacked, mouth wide open and well armed with long, sharp teeth. I talk to animals, especially when they are very angry. It often calms them down a bit. It also calms me down a lot. The female stopped three feet (1 m) from me, glared, snarled again and lunged, then turned abruptly and undulated back to her pup.

The pup was lovely. It looked small and slim next to its massive, 400-pound (180 kg) mother. Actually, compared with other seal pups, most of whom are fatless at birth, the hooded seal pup is born wrapped in a cozy blubber blanket that makes up 19 percent of its birth weight of forty-eight pounds (22 kg). The pup was slightly more than three feet (1 m) long and clad in a most elegant short-haired coat: deep bluish-gray above, shading into silvery gray and creamy white on sides and belly. (These are the "blueback" pelts so highly prized by sealers, for they can be made into very expensive fur coats for rich ladies.)

Fat and full, a hooded seal pup rests between meals.

The pup was only half an hour old, but it wasted no time. It cried and nudged its mother. She rolled onto her side; the pup suckled urgently, eyes closed in blissful concentration, and switched frequently from teat to teat. After about ten minutes, the pup stopped nursing, its blue-black muzzle flecked with cream, mewled contentedly, yawned and fell asleep. In about half an hour it awoke, butted its mother and began to nurse again. And so it went, from early morning when the pup was born until evening when we had to leave.

Day two. The mother is less hostile and her pup a lot fatter. Since yesterday, it has gained fifteen pounds (7 kg). The female has also acquired a suitor, a young male with high hopes and nary a chance. A female will drive off any male until she comes into estrus. Top males know this and do not waste their time waiting and hoping. They cruise the ice, searching for receptive females, drive off local suitors of inferior rank, mate and set out for other conquests.

Day three. The female ignores me; she is used to my presence. She has acquired another suitor, an older male that dislikes me and attacks. But all I have to do is step into the female's private sphere and she attacks—not me, but the pursuing male; he meekly turns and flees. The pup has gained another fifteen pounds (7 kg). It is beginning to look globular.

Day four. The pup is obese. It has gained about sixty pounds (27 kg) since it was born. It looks like a furry blimp with flippers. But it still drinks with the same desperate urgency, sleeps and drinks, sleeps and drinks, and gets fatter by the minute. It is an extraordinarily efficient energy transfer from mother to pup: in four days the pup has more than doubled its birth weight, and the mother has lost about eighty pounds (36 kg), near-ly all in blubber. Mother's blubber now enfolds her bloated baby.

Day five. It's over. Yesterday the female allowed me, without anger, to come within ten feet (3 m) of her and her pup, but not closer. Today I can touch the pup. She lies three feet (1 m) from me and the pup and does not show the slightest interest in either of us. Her task is done. The pup, a globular lump of barely mobile blubber, knows it. Wheezing, it makes a halfhearted attempt to nurse, is rebuffed and falls asleep. Two powerful males hover in attendance; their time is nigh. They bite and slash with sharp-clawed fore flip-pers, inflate their hoods, blow out their septums. Toward noon, the female moves slowly away, the bigger of the two bulls follows her, and soon they will mate.

The pup remains, thickly wrapped in blubber, its mother's legacy. I sit with it, stroke its lovely fur and talk to it. It opens its eyes, looks blankly at me, sighs deeply and falls asleep. Over the next several weeks it will sleep most of the time, expending a minimum of energy, living off that precious blubber, using less than two pounds (1 kg) a day, until in late April the ice disintegrates and the pup, having used up slightly more than half its blubber reserve, goes to sea and begins to feed itself.

In four days the hooded seal pup is weaned. It is now so fat it can barely move.

BACK FROM THE BRINK: THE RETURN OF THE NORTHERN ELEPHANT SEAL

*I*N 1880, THE NORTHERN ELEPHANT SEAL, mightiest of all seals with the exception of its close relative, the southern elephant seal, was considered extinct. For seventy years it had been ruthlessly killed, and colony after colony had been exterminated. In 1880, hunters discovered the last colony: 400 elephant seals on a sheltered beach of Baja California near Isla Cedros. All were shot or clubbed to death. The giant seal, it was assumed, was now extinct.

The elephant seal is "one of the bygone wonders of the animal world."
—AN AMERICAN BIOLOGY BOOK, 1884

In 1892, rumors reached Charles Haskins Townsend of the Smithsonian Institution that a few elephant seals might survive on a remote, uninhabited island far out in the Pacific, Mexico-owned Isla de Guadalupe, 150 miles (240 km) west of Baja California. He organized an expedition, found eight elephant seals on a small, crescent-shaped beach—and promptly shot seven of them because "few, if any, specimens were to be found in the museums of North America."

That was the northern elephant seal's nadir. Scientists estimate that between twenty and a hundred animals (out of an original population of 100,000) survived the slaughter, perhaps at sea, perhaps in Guadalupe's jagged lava caves. (These caves also provided sanctuary to the last Guadalupe fur seals. Once numerous and widespread, they, too, were hunted to near extinction in the nineteenth century. They now number about 2,500.)

Before other museum hunters could "clean up" this remnant, the California Academy of Sciences intervened. At its urging, President Alvaro Obregón of Mexico gave total protection to the *elefante marino*, and in 1922 declared Isla de Guadalupe a wildlife

The northern elephant seal owes its name to its size, and to the nearly half yard (almost .5 m) long, inflatable proboscis of the male.

reserve. Mexico took a no-nonsense attitude to conservation: a squad of soldiers was posted on the island with orders "to shoot anyone molesting the animals."

At the beginning of the nineteenth century, the northern elephant seal bred from Cabo San Lázaro, near the southern tip of Baja California, to Point Reyes, just north of San Francisco, a distance of slightly more than 990 miles (1,600 km). The original population exceeded 100,000 animals living mainly on offshore islands.

Russian hunters began the slaughter in 1810 (at that time Russia owned a small part of California), and soon Spanish and then American "elephanters" joined the fray. "A fat bull," recorded the sealer-whaler-naturalist Charles Scammon in 1874, "yielded 210 gallons of oil," enough to fuel one lamp for four years. The oil was also used in tanning, to lubricate machinery, waterproof garments, fuel the streetlights of America and for paints and soaps. In 1840, it sold for one dollar a gallon.

The huge, lethargic seals were easy to kill: elephanters stampeded them away from the beach, then shot, clubbed or lanced them at leisure. The historian Briton Cooper Busch has estimated that elephanters killed about 250,000 northern elephant seals between 1810 and 1860.

After total protection for the pitiful remnant, initially by Mexico and then also by the United States, the elephant seals increased, slowly at first, then with amazing rapidity. For a long time they clung to the security of Guadalupe Island, but as its beaches became too crowded, they spread and began to recolonize islands they had inhabited a

In the 1880s, less than 100 northern elephant seals survived. With protection, they have recovered. Here, the large colony on San Miguel Island, California. ▶

long time ago: in 1918, the Islas San Benito off Baja California; 1925, San Miguel, one of California's Channel Islands; in 1951, the Farallon Islands near San Francisco. Their numbers grew to 1,500 in 1930; to 13,000 in 1957; to 48,000 in 1976; to 70,000 in 1984. Today, about 120,000 northern elephant seals, roughly the prehunt population, occupy their entire former range.

Young male elephant seals are usually the travelers and initial colonizers. Typically, about five years after they settle on an empty island beach, the first females follow and a colony is established. In recent years some young males have wandered far: they are now sighted every year off the coast of British Columbia, where their strange shape, soulful eyes and lugubrious sighs have given rise to tales of mermaids. A few were recently seen off Alaska. And during lunchtime on April 25, 1985, a young elephant seal bull climbed the pier at a San Francisco yacht club and, reported the *San Francisco Chronicle*, "waddled up China Basin Street … creating an instant traffic jam."

All 120,000 northern elephant seals today may be the descendants of one single male, the Adam of their species. Since these seals are polygamous, that last little herd on Guadalupe Island may have been ruled by one alpha bull, the Grand Sire of all northern elephant seals. They have, in consequence, great genetic homogeneity. When Burney J. LeBoeuf of the University of California at Santa Cruz, foremost expert on elephant seals, took blood samples from many seals, he found them to be as similar as are the blood samples of identical twins.

Young northern elephant seal threatening. ▶

Yet as the seals spread to far-flung colonies, they developed distinctive regional traits. LeBoeuf discovered that the elephant seals now "speak regional dialects," an evolutionary achievement once thought to be confined only to a few bird species and to humans.

The rhythmic, resonant, metallic calls of the males, which can be heard for nearly a mile and a quarter (2 km), vary considerably in pulse rate, pitch, intensity and timbre. The animals of a rookery recognize one another perhaps by sight, but definitely by voice. Each island group is now developing its own dialect; it gives cohesion and distinctiveness to their group. Seals from afar first seem confused by the local lingo, then either leave or settle down and adopt it.

I visited San Miguel Island several times with marine mammal expert Brent S. Stewart of the Hubbs Marine Research Center in San Diego. The great bulls had arrived on the breeding beaches in early December full of ambition, energy and fat. Their blubber layer at this time is up to six inches (14 cm) thick and constitutes about 40 percent of their total weight.

The fights of these master bulls are awesome spectacles. Despite their length (16 feet/5 m), bulk and weight (2 tons/1 800 kg), the giant bulls can be amazingly flexible and agile. They rear high, like Brobdingnagian cobras, and hack and slash at each other's necks and chests with lightning speed and long, yellow canines. Soon blood streams from the fighting males. The fights are fierce but seldom fatal, because a thick, deeply wrinkled chest shield of cornified tissue protects the antagonists.

The winners of these mighty, primal battles rule over sections of beach and the females upon it, and turn, in the words of one observer, into "sex-obsessed mating machines." Being alpha bull has its perks, but it is not an easy life. A top bull fights often,

Battle of the giants. Furious northern elephant seal bulls rear and hack at each other with daggerlike canines. Combatants bleed profusely, but severe injuries are rare.

Holding his female firmly with trunk and flipper, a northern elephant seal bull mates.

A hungry northern elephant seal pup calls loudly for its mother.

Largest of all seals, a southern elephant seal lies on a beach of the Falkland Islands.

does not eat or drink for up to three months, mates frequently and rarely sleeps. "For about 1^1/$_2$ months, he must be potent, fertile and willing—again and again," writes LeBoeuf. "A better system for selecting the fittest males to perpetuate the species would be difficult to imagine."

Their reign is exalted, strenuous and brief. Most last only one season; they plummet from alpha to omega and never breed again. Having lost 1,500 pounds (675 kg), nearly half their weight, in three frenzied months, they crawl into the sea, gaunt, battered hulks, easy prey for the killer whales and great white sharks that normally feed on young animals.

The females, only one-third as heavy as the colossal males, are round and padded with blubber when they arrive on the beaches to give birth to their dark-furred eighty-pound (36 kg) pups. The pups, fed on fat-rich milk, balloon to about 300 pounds (135 kg) in four weeks, then gather in chummy "weaner pods" and sleep.

Some elephant seal females are kind to strange pups and let them nurse alongside their own. These milk moochers make the rounds and grow even fatter than normal pups. A few very tolerant cows are surrounded by hopeful pups. I watched one female nurse two, while eight others waited their turn.

Occasionally, an extremely fortunate pup has, in addition to its own mother, a foster parent, either a female that has lost her pup or a nearby female that tolerates a second feeder for the entire lactation period. With a double dose of the enormously rich milk, such pups turn into "superweaners," blimplike creatures that weigh about 600 pounds (270 kg). These fortunate and pushy pups are nearly always males. With a head start over others of their age group, they have a good chance to reign, in ten to twelve years, for one glorious summer as alpha bulls, probably upon the beach where they were born.

Weaned, fat and friendly, southern elephant seal pups seek one another's company.

Southern Giants

The northern elephant seal is large; the southern elephant seal is larger—the largest of all pinnipeds. Top males are more than sixteen feet (5 m) long and weigh about four tons—8,000 pounds (3,600 kg)! For all its monstrous size, it is even more flexible than its northern cousin: it can rear up, then twist backward until its head touches its rear flippers, forming a perfect O—quite a feat for a four-ton gymnast!

The northern elephant seal lives off California, the southern on subantarctic islands. The southern male has a bulbous but short schnozzle. The northern male has a splendid, nearly foot and a half (.5 m) long pendulous proboscis, an elephantine trunk that, when he is excited, he can inflate, to impress a rival and perhaps use as a resonating chamber for his metallic-sounding trumpet calls.

Elephanters nearly wiped out the northern elephant seal. They also killed more than one million southern elephant seals, often as a sideline to the frenzied nineteenth-century fur seal hunt or to whaling. The great seals were slaughtered, flayed, their blubber rendered into oil, their carcasses abandoned. Although hunted until the 1960s, the southern elephant seals were never butchered to the edge of extinction. Sufficient stock remained on most breeding islands for the species to recover, and they now number about 600,000.

I watched them on Sea Lion Island just south of the main group of Falkland Islands, where I spent part of an austral summer. The breeding season was over; most adult males and females had left the beaches to hunt at sea and replenish their badly depleted blubber reserves. Weaned pups played and began to explore, cautiously, the sea. Young males jousted. They reared up just as the big bulls do, looked fierce, heaved, pushed and grunted with exertion, but did not hurt each other.

Some seals had already returned for their annual molt, another strenuous phase in an elephant seal's life. All seals molt, and to molt they must haul out onto land or ice and fast and suffer. The old fur looks drab and worn. The skin is scabrous and itchy. The seals are listless, tired. They itch, they scratch, they sleep. Small flakes of skin and hair peel off and litter ice or beach. After three weeks or a month, elegant in glossy new fur, the seals slip into the sea to feed voraciously after their long fast.

In elephant seals the molt is more dramatic: they slough off the entire epidermal layer, skin and hair, in large, moldy-looking patches. It's an exhausting process, and elephant seals, lethargic at the best of times, now become nearly comatose. To conserve heat (and energy) they usually lie close together, as they slowly peel from nose to tail.

This is of interest to several opportunistic birds. The pure-white sheathbill, an odd bird of the Far South that looks like a cross between a gull and pigeon, is primarily a scavenger and cautiously picks up the bits and pieces that fall off the sleeping giants. The little, brownish tussock bird, native to the Falklands and Tierra del Fuego, is already more adventurous. It flutters up to the sleeping behemoths and chips off bits of flaking skin or pecks dried mucus from a seal's nose.

Boldest is the striated caracara, the rowdy pirate of these islands. Normally raucous and fluffy-feathered, this long-legged, powerful raptor looks sleeky, sneaky, lean and mean as it approaches the sleeping molting elephant seals. Not content with pickings, the hook-beaked bird tiptoes close, looks for a good spot, darts in, and *rip*—there goes a piece of skin. The great seal wakes, roars ineffectually, falls asleep, and the caracara sidles in to get another chunk of skin.

These are the minor annoyances of elephant seal life. A real danger to them, as to seals in so many other regions, is overfishing by the fleets of many nations in the southern oceans. Most southern elephant seal colonies have not yet suffered, but those on the Falkland Islands are decreasing in number. The Falkland Island artist-naturalist Tony Chater, with whom I lived for a while on New Island, writes sadly in his beautiful book *The Falklands* that although the great fishing fleets have brought prosperity to the Falkland Islands, they have also brought "paucity and pollution to Falkland beaches. The magnificent sea elephants are rapidly replaced along the shore by rusty oil drums, lengths of bright green fishing net and plastic detergent bottles."

A tussock bird pecks flaking skin off a molting southern elephant seal in the Falkland Islands.

A warning roar that means little. The large, lethargic southern elephant seals would rather sleep than fight. ▶

PART IV

THE WALRUS

◄ *Walruses like togetherness. Here, they lie in cozy and malodorous heaps upon an Alaskan beach.*

I THE WONDROUS WALRUS

VORY. ALONG WITH GOLD, RUBIES AND DIAMONDS it is one of the substances most desired by humans. King Solomon, says the Bible, had "a great throne of ivory." In Moscow's Armory, the treasury of Russia's tsars, stands the Ivory Throne of Tsar Ivan the Terrible. In St. Petersburg, in the Peter Gallery of the Hermitage, hangs the great ivory chandelier that Tsar Peter the Great himself carved in 1693 from walrus ivory in Arkhangelsk while waiting for supply ships from Holland.

Giles Fletcher, Queen Elizabeth I's ambassador to Russia, reported in 1588 in detail on the wealth of that country. Among its most valuable exports were the ivory tusks of "a fish called Morse" that lives in the arctic seas. "Its teeth are of great value and the Persians and Bougharians fetch it from thence for beads, knife handles and sword hafts of Noblemen." When the American scientist and ivory specialist Richard Ettinghausen examined some years ago fifty sword and dagger handles from ancient Persia and Turkey, now in U.S. collections, he found "that most handles were fashioned from the tusks of the walrus."

When I did the research for my book about the narwhal and its wonder-working, spiraled ivory tusk, I found that the ancient trade routes that brought narwhal ivory to the great lands of wealth of the early medieval world—China, India, Arabia and some of the courts of Europe—paralleled those that brought walrus ivory to the same destinations. It was transported from Viking-settled Greenland to the papal see: a papal bull of 1282 states that Greenland was to pay its tithes to the papal see in walrus ivory and sealskins. It was transported from eastern Siberia—and from Alaska long before

Walrus ivory, al-khutu, *is "the tooth of a fish one cubit long which the Volga Bulgars bring from the northern sea. It is sent to Mecca and to the Egyptians who crave it … They make from it sword and knife handles.*
—ABU RAYHAN MUHAMMAD IBN AHMAD AL-BIRUNI, ARAB SCHOLAR AND TRAVELER, 973–1048, IN HIS BOOK ON MINERALOGY, WRITTEN A THOUSAND YEARS AGO

The walrus's Latin name, **Odobenus,** *means "tooth walker." It uses its tusks to haul out onto slippery ice floes.*

Columbus—to China, where the Chinese author, scholar and near-contemporary of al-Biruni, Hung Hao, praised it in A.D. 1095 as "a priceless jewel." And it was transported from all of arctic Russia and Siberia, along exceedingly complex routes, by dog team, horse and camel caravans to the ancient oasis city of Khiva in the Kyzyl-Kum Desert of Central Asia, which was, a thousand years ago, the walrus-ivory center of the world.

Khiva still exists. My wife and I lived there as in a dream of long ago. It is one of those rare places, like Carcassonne in France and Rothenburg ob der Tauber in Germany, miraculously preserved, spared the devastations of wars, disasters and progress, an ancient city in the desert that time forgot. There the ivory tusks from the remote north were transformed by master craftsmen in vaulted shops, some of which still exist, into beads, lovely combs, elaborate filigree brooches and, mainly, into magnificent hafts for swords, knives and daggers. Then other caravans took these precious carvings to Persia and India, to the great centers of wealth and learning of the Arab world—Damascus, Baghdad and Alexandria—and to the Alhambra, the great castle of the Moorish kings in Spain.

The trade in walrus ivory was immense. On a reduced scale, it continues to this day. But whereas for gold, rubies and diamonds people slaved, for ivory animals died, among them the walrus, one of the most fascinating members of the pinniped tribe.

The walrus, literally whale-horse, from the Old Norse *hvalr* (whale) and *rosm* (horse), comes in two versions: A and P, Atlantic and Pacific. The Atlantic walrus, weighing up to a ton (900 kg), lives along the arctic coasts of Siberia, Russia, Greenland and the eastern Canadian Arctic. The Pacific walrus, larger, more massive, with much longer, thicker tusks, lives mainly in the Bering Sea and migrates in summer northward through Bering Strait into the Chukchi Sea as far as ice will allow.

A walrus with an itchy back rubs and rolls on an ice floe.

A massive and majestic walrus bull in Alaska rears up.

In historic times, the greatest walrus colonies were not in the Arctic but far south: on Sable Island in the Atlantic, a hundred miles (160 km) east of Nova Scotia, and on the Magdalen Islands in the Gulf of St. Lawrence. (During cold periods of the Pleistocene, walruses ranged even farther south and basked on the beaches of South Carolina and the Bay of Biscay.) In 1641, hunters from Boston obtained "four hundred pairs of seahorse teeth" on Sable Island, and by the end of the seventeenth century that colony had been exterminated.

The walrus colonies on the Magdalen Islands were much larger and lasted longer. King Louis XIV of France bestowed, in feudal fashion, *la pêche aux vaches marines*, as he called it, "the sea cow fishery," on wealthy or worthy subjects. And from the island, year after year, came ships with walrus products: skins cut into thong, for purposes as varied as mooring hawsers or hauling up giant stones to build Cologne's cathedral (walrus thong was, according to the anthropologist Froelich Rainey, "the strongest line known before the invention of the steel cable"); tusks for anything from crucifixes to combs; and oil for soaps, candles and the lamps of Europe. In 300 years, hundreds of thousands of walruses were butchered on the Magdalen Islands. The last one died in the spring of 1799.

Walruses, like bearded seals, are bottom feeders: they like the shallow northern seas above the continental shelf. They dive to a maximum depth of 330 feet (100 m), but preferably much less, and eat anything edible that's down there: sea cucumbers, starfish, shrimps and crabs, although they prefer whelks, mussels, cockles and clams.

It had long been assumed that walruses rake up shellfish with their tusks, crush them and eat them. But the tusks do not show wear, tuskless walruses are fat, and you hardly ever find a clam shell in a walrus stomach. Scientists now speculate that the walrus dives

headfirst to the sea bottom, where it roots in the muck like a pig searching for truffles. It detects shellfish with its 400-odd quill-like vibrissae, which are set in highly innervated sensitive mystacial pads. Then it creates a powerful sucking action with its tongue, enfolds clams with strong, mobile lips, snaps off the siphons, or feet, or sucks out the entire animal. A sort of submarine vacuum cleaner, the efficient walrus slurps in energy-rich clams for about ten minutes, surfaces, breathes and dives again for the next course.

Walruses have a prodigious appetite: an adult eats about 100 pounds (45 kg) of food a day—that's the meat of about 800 soft-shell clams or 10,000 of the smaller hard-shell clams. Inuit hunters open the stomachs of killed animals and scoop out the partially digested clams; they are a favorite food. Having lived with Inuit for so many years, I've eaten these clams often: they taste like oysters with kick; the digestive juices give them a tart vinegary flavor.

Whereas bottom-dwelling creatures are the diet of the vast majority of walruses, a few live on meat. These are the "killer," or "rogue," walruses that figure prominently in the lore of Inuit from Siberia to Greenland. They are waifs, according to the Inuit, animals that lost their mothers while still young. To survive they fed on carrion. Doing so, they developed a taste for blubber and meat, and began to kill and eat seals.

The appearance of a rogue walrus is distinctive. The shoulders and forelimbs appear unusually large and powerfully developed; chin, throat, chest and tusks are amber colored because of the oxidized seal oil. Their tusks, twin ivory stilettos, are long, slender and sharp. A rogue walrus, say the Inuit, swims quietly up to a sleeping seal, enfolds it

◀ *A powerful Pacific walrus bull surfaces near Round Island, Alaska.*

with his powerful front flippers, crushes it, rips the skin with its tusks and sucks off all the blubber and some of the meat. The rogue walrus lives alone. Walruses, generally, are compulsively gregarious. But they fear and shun the rogue.

The livers of rogue walruses, like those of the primarily blubber-eating polar bear, contain exceedingly high amounts of vitamin A. When eaten by humans, the livers of such walruses can cause severe poisoning or even death due to hypervitaminosis. Rogue walruses, again like polar bears, are also likely to be infested with the parasite trichinae. In 1947 in Greenland, 300 people contracted trichinosis after eating such walrus meat and 33 died. Rogue walruses are rare, about one in a thousand, according to Alaska's foremost walrus expert, Francis H. Fay.

Apart from man, walruses have few enemies. They are immensely powerful animals. The long tusks of males and females are deadly weapons, and when threatened, walruses attack in concert; an entire herd will charge in fury upon the enemy. Even the mighty killer whales prefer not to tackle infuriated walruses. When a Polar Inuk of northwest Greenland is hunting in his frail kayak and is surprised far from shore by killer whales, he cups his hands and bellows into the water, imitating the roar of an enraged walrus bull. The sound travels far in water, and Inuit hunters have told me that the killer whales promptly veer off.

Walruses woo and mate in winter, usually in March. Females rest on an ice pan, and around the pan swims a large bull walrus that "sings": his repertoire is small and repetitive but unusual. He starts with a series of rapid clacking noises, like castanets, either by clacking his teeth or, more likely, by powerful, staccato glottal plosives. He then produces, most strange coming from such a massive, warty animal, a sound of exquisite

*Tusk size determines rank in walrus society. Angry Pacific walrus bulls rear up
and flash their massive ivory tusks at each other.*

beauty: the clear, resonant chiming of bells, the sound amplified by the male's basket-ball-sized pharyngeal air pouches on either side of the upper neck. Finally the bull surfaces near the edge of the floe, puckers his fat, mobile lips and whistles, so shrill you can hear it a mile and a quarter (2 km) away.

The result of all this wooing is, after a year's gestation, a slightly more than 3 feet (1 m) long, 120-pound (54 kg) calf the size of an adult ringed seal, born on an ice floe. It is covered with a coat of short, silvery gray hairs, which are exchanged for rusty brown ones after the postnatal molt.

The mother-calf bond in walruses is extremely strong; for about two years, they are nearly inseparable. In cold weather she hugs the calf to her chest, cradling it with her broad, nearly foot and a half (.5 m) long front flippers to keep it warm. When swimming, the calf rides on its mother's neck like a plump little marine jockey, clasping it firmly with its rough-soled flippers. When danger threatens, the female sweeps her calf off the floe, holds it to her chest with her flippers and dives. She defends it valiantly and, even when severely wounded, does not abandon it. The high-pitched, desperate barking of a calf not only arouses its mother to furious protectiveness, but also impels nearby wal-ruses to rush to its defense. Thus, although the reproductive rate of walruses is low, with cows bearing calves at two- to three-year intervals, calf survival, due to intense maternal care, is high.

Most walruses migrate. Those that spent the winter off West Greenland swim far to the north in summer to the rich shellfish banks in the shallow seas between Ellesmere Island and northern Greenland. Most of the Pacific population, including nearly all females, calves and immature animals, swim north through Bering Strait and scatter over

Using a traditional bow drill, an Inuit carver in Alaska makes a bracelet from walrus ivory.

For Inuit hunting in kayaks, walruses could be dangerous adversaries. In this print by the Cape Dorset artist Pudlo Pudlat, the mighty walrus wins. The print's title is **The Last Hunt.**

the immense, shallow and food-rich Chukchi Sea, thereby diminishing the pressure on their food resources. Their needs are enormous. If one walrus eats 10,000 hard-shell clams a day, the world's 300,000 walruses would consume, if all were feeding, three trillion clams a day. They don't, of course. Typically, they dive frequently and eat for a day or two, then rest and digest for several days. There is some indication that the siphons they snip off clams, a major part of their diet, are regenerated by the clams, so to some extent these mollusks are a renewable harvest.

Although most walruses migrate, many males do not. They gather at a traditional hauling-out place called an *ugli* (plural *uglit*) by the Inuit. Unless exterminated or continually disturbed, walruses will return to the same *ugli* for years. Seahorse Point on Southampton Island in Hudson Bay was given its name in 1615 by the explorer William Baffin because he saw large numbers of walruses there. Walruses haul out at the same spot today. (To avoid disturbing and perhaps chasing away the animals that were so precious to them, Inuit in the past had a taboo against hunting walruses on an *ugli* or in its vicinity.)

There are several large *uglit* with thousands of male walruses on the Siberian coast of the Bering Sea and some on the Alaskan. The most famous *ugli* is on Round Island in Bristol Bay, where as many as 12,000 walruses gather and where I spent a part of two summers, endlessly fascinated by these gregarious yet disputatious animals that carpet some of the beaches until they are wall-to-wall walruses.

After a storm, when most walruses leave the wave-lashed beaches for a while, or when they have been panicked into the sea by a low-flying aircraft (forbidden, but it happens), a few sleep vertically in the water near the island, buoyed by their inflated pharyngeal pouches, while most swim back and forth along the shore, loath to haul out on an empty beach. Usually an old massive bull makes the first move. Wheezing and snorting, he laboriously drags his two-ton (1,800 kg) bulk onto the beach. He pauses frequently and appears apprehensive. At this time, the warning cry of a gull can send him back into the sea. (When established on the beach walruses sleep so soundly scientists have taken their temperature rectally without waking them.) Once the great male has found a congenial spot and goes to sleep, his presence acts as magnet to other walruses.

Slowly, with much grunting and groaning, the walruses reoccupy the beach. They like togetherness but spacing is hierarchical: the most powerful lie in the center, the younger, weaker animals on the periphery. Bulk, power and, above all, tusk size determine social status. A bull with broken, shortened tusks slips way down the social ladder. Walruses jab and jostle, hack downward and sideways with a speed surprising in animals so bulky. A walrus's skin, two inches (5 cm) thick, is extremely tough and injuries are rare, but twice I saw walruses that had lost an eye.

Finally, the walruses settle down in an accepted order of precedence and do what walruses most enjoy: they sleep, a dense, miasmic mass, "exuding nauseous smell," as Homer said nearly 3,000 years ago in the *Odyssey*.

"What would happen," I asked biologist friends in Alaska, "if I joined walruses in shallow water near their hauling beach?" Opinions diverged: a few thought the walruses would attack ("You'll be a smear upon the rocks," said one); most said they would flee.

On a rare nice, quiet day at Round Island I put on hip waders, eased into the water behind a shielding rock and crept cautiously toward a group of walruses lolling in the

Inuit hunters cut up shot walruses upon an ice floe in Bering Strait.

shallows thirty feet (10 m) away. It took the great bulls a while to realize I was there and that I wasn't a fellow walrus. They stared at me with slightly protuberant bloodshot eyes, baffled and affronted like elderly club men who have been disturbed; then they wheezed and harrumphed and swam closer for a better look. They stopped barely six feet (2 m) from me and we looked at each other in mutual wonder. Just then I slipped on an algae-coated rock, moved abruptly, and the spell was broken. The walruses turned and fled.

PART V

AFTERTHOUGHTS

◀ *Seals for human amusement: a trained harbor seal performs at the aquarium in Quebec City, Canada.*

OF SEALS AND MEN

*I*NUTERSSUAQ OF THE POLAR INUIT was a born teacher. A man of great dignity, a famous hunter and traveler, he enjoyed sharing the knowledge and wisdom of a long life. After dinner (usually seal), we sat in the soft light of the arctic night in his simple home in Siorapaluk, the northernmost village on earth, and Inuterssuaq, picking his words very carefully, for he knew that my knowledge of his language was limited, unfolded for me the past of his people.

For that which befalleth the sons of men befalleth beasts … as the one dieth, so dieth the other; yea, they have all one breath; so that man hath no preeminence above a beast.
—OLD TESTAMENT
(ECCLESIASTES 3:19)

He spoke of hunting walrus on thin ice, of making baleen snares to capture arctic hares, of the ingenious traps they built to catch foxes, of the endless hours spent waiting for seals to surface.

He explained to me in detail the hunting techniques that had enabled his people to live in a land so harsh, where the average temperature of only one month, July, is above the freezing point and winter's darkness, day and night, lasts from October to February.

And he tried to explain to me the ethos of his people, who once had been as one with nature and its animals; who ate animals but respected them; to whom, in ages past, to waste an animal had been taboo, for it was an offense against the *inua*, "the spirit of the animal."

One night I asked him, "What is the most important thing in life?" He reflected for a while, his dark, weather-sculptured face solemn, and then he smiled and said, "Seals, for without them we could not live."

Walrus skulls and bones, remnants of long-ago meals, lie near a prehistoric Inuit house on Coats Island in Hudson Bay. ▶

As Dionyse Settle, the Elizabethan chronicler of the explorer Martin Frobisher's second expedition to Baffin Island, so shrewdly observed in 1577, in the first detailed description of Inuit: "Those beastes, flesh, fishes and fowles, which they kil, they are meate, drinke, apparel, houses, bedding, hose, shoos, thred, saile for their boates … and almost all their riches." The seal did, in fact, make the Arctic habitable: for the Inuit the seal was life, and their greatest goddess was Sedna, mother of seals and whales.

Like all predators, the Inuit and other coastal people in Siberia, arctic Russia and in Europe who hunted seals lived in balance with their prey. That ancient balance was broken when humans killed pinnipeds (and other animals) in large numbers for a multitude of reasons: fun and sport; commerce and profit; to eliminate them as competitors in the harvest of the sea's wealth.

The Romans were a marvelously ingenious people, and they expended a fair amount of that genius devising novel methods for killing humans and animals for the amusement of princes and plebs. The Circus Maximus (seating capacity 350,000) could be flooded for bloody sea battles. "Fights" were also staged between polar bears and seals (probably the now nearly extinct Mediterranean monk seal): *A equoreos ego cum certantibus ursi spectavi vitulos* . . . wrote the Roman poet Calpurnius in A.D. 57. ("Sea calves also I beheld with bears pitted against them").

Christopher Columbus, on his second voyage, anchored in August 1594 off Alta Vela Island south of Haiti and killed eight "sea wolves" that were sleeping on the beach. Later, the pirate-cum-explorer-naturalist William Dampier remarked in 1675, "The Spaniards do often come hither to make Oyl of their Fat." That was the Caribbean monk seal. The last one was seen in 1952. It is now officially listed as extinct.

A female Steller sea lion in Alaska.

The Little Mermaid in Copenhagen, Denmark.

In the 1800s, wealthy European "sportsmen" hired Norwegian sealing vessels for £800 sterling (a British servant's wage at the time was £12 sterling a year) to hunt sea mammals in the seas north of Norway and Russia. "There we hunt the walrus, the narwhal, and the seal, / Aha! 't was a noble game," wrote the American poet Henry Wadsworth Longfellow. Today rich "sportsmen" pay $10,000 to $20,000 to kill walruses off Alaska.

The peak of pinniped killing came in the nineteenth century as hundreds of ships roamed the oceans of the world to kill fur seals, sea lions, walruses, elephant seals and harp and hooded seals in the millions, sometimes at the rate of a million a year. The great hunts ceased because few animals remained or the last colonies were too small and too remote to make commercial trips profitable.

Today, though more limited, the killing of seals continues: fur seals in Uruguay and Namibia, Caspian seals in Russia and Kazakhstan, hooded seals on the ice off Canada and Greenland. In Canada, under government-set quotas, more than a quarter million harp seals are killed annually.

But the killing, while repellent to many, does not endanger the survival of a single seal species today. Pollution and overfishing endanger many, perhaps most, pinniped species.

A mere century ago, the seas of the world were unbelievably rich. "It has been calculated," wrote Alexandre Dumas in *Le Grand Dictionnaire de Cuisine* in 1873, "that if no accident prevented the hatching of the eggs and each egg reached maturity, it would only take three years to fill the sea so that you could walk across the Atlantic dryshod on the backs of cod."

We may allow some hyperbole to the author of *The Three Musketeers* and *The Count of*

Monte Cristo, but serious scientists believed the sea's wealth to be inexhaustible. Three thousand years ago, Homer, in the *Odyssey*, sang the praise of "the fish-full sea." The famous English biologist Thomas Henry Huxley agreed: "I believe probably all the great sea fisheries are inexhaustible: that is to say, nothing we do seriously affects the number of fish." And in 1885, Canada's Ministry of Agriculture confidently predicted, "Unless the order of nature is overthrown, for centuries to come our fisheries will continue to be fertile."

They could have been, but we have overthrown and disregarded "the order of nature," and in less than a century, we have devastated the "unlimited" fish stocks of the world. We took the factory to sea and methodically destroyed the cod, the capelin, the anchoveta. We encircled miles of sea with nets and hauled in tuna, dolphins, seals, sea turtles and seabirds in millions. We "cleaned out" an ocean area and moved on to the next, the way nineteenth-century fur seal hunters moved from island to island killing all seals "because if we don't kill them someone else will," and finally it all collapsed because there were no more seals. Pollution and the worldwide uncontrolled rape of the sea are now the greatest danger to all sea mammals, including the seals of the world.

◄   *To Inuit, seals were life. They made their existence in the Arctic possible.*
A Polar Inuk of northwest Greenland hunts ringed seals at the floe edge.

A Polar Inuit woman chews bearded seal leather, the tough sole of a sealskin boot.

Victim of oceans full of discarded, long-lasting strangling nets: a Cape fur seal in Namibia.

L'Envoi

I HAVE LIVED WITH SEALS NOW for thirty-five years; my life, as a shamanistic prophecy accurately predicted more than forty years ago, has indeed been "rich in seals."

I am evidently partial to the tribe. Watching their lives for months, for years, has deepened my understanding of the miraculous diversity and perfection of nature. The English poet, artist and mystic William Blake wrote 200 years ago in his *Auguries of Innocence*:

> To see the world in a grain of sand,
>
> And heaven in a wild flower;
>
> Hold infinity in the palm of your hand,
>
> And eternity in an hour.

In seals, and other animals, I see the wonder of nature, the marvel of Creation, and I hope for a new human ethos, an understanding that we are not a race apart but a part of this universal web of nature, that each time we kill needlessly, heedlessly, we diminish not only Nature but ourselves and the world we leave to coming generations.

We seem to have a choice: we can have a world aswarm with billions of humans, plus rats and cockroaches and little else, or, with love and care and caution, we can maintain the world in all its marvelous diversity.

> Accuse not Nature she has done her part;
>
> Do thou but thine.
>
> —John Milton, *Paradise Lost*

Innocents in Paradise. Hooker's sea lion pups on the remote,
uninhabited Auckland Islands of New Zealand.

Fred Bruemmer communes with a harp seal upon the Gulf of St. Lawrence ice.

THE PINNIPED TRIBE

SEALS OF THE WORLD

FAMILY: OTARIIDAE (the Eared Seals)

FUR SEALS (9 species)

1. Northern, or Alaska, Fur Seal (*Callorhinus ursinus*)
2. New Zealand Fur Seal (*Arctocephalus forsteri*)
3. Cape, or South African, Fur Seal (*Arctocephalus pusillus*)
4. Antarctic Fur Seal (*Arctocephalus gazella*)
5. Subantarctic Fur Seal (*Arctocephalus tropicalis*)
6. South American Fur Seal (*Arctocephalus australis*)
7. Juan Fernandez Fur Seal (*Arctocephalus philippii*)
8. Galápagos Fur Seal (*Arctocephalus galápagoensis*)
9. Guadalupe Fur Seal (*Arctocephalus townsendi*)

SEA LIONS (5 species)

1. Steller, or Northern, Sea Lion (*Eumetopias jubatus*)
2. California Sea Lion (*Zalophus californianus*)
3. Southern Sea Lion (*Otaria byronia*)
4. Australian Sea lion (*Neophoca cinera*)
5. Hooker's Sea Lion (*Phocarctos hookeri*)

FAMILY: PHOCIDAE (the Earless, or True, Seals)

MONK SEALS (2 species)

1. Mediterranean Monk Seal (*Monachus monachus*)
2. Hawaiian Monk Seal (*Monachus schauinslandi*)

NORTHERN SEALS (10 species)

1. Gray Seal (*Halichoerus grypus*)
2. Harbor, or Common, Seal (*Phoca vitulina*)
3. Largha Seal (*Phoca largha*)
4. Ringed Seal (*Phoca hispida*)
5. Caspian Seal (*Phoca caspica*)
6. Baikal Seal (*Phoca sibirica*)
7. Harp Seal (*Phoca groenlandica*)
8. Ribbon Seal (*Phoca fasciata*)
9. Hooded Seal (*Cystophora cristata*)
10. Bearded Seal (*Erignathus barbatus*)

ANTARCTIC SEALS (4 species)

1. Weddell Seal (*Leptonychotes weddelli*)
2. Ross Seal (*Ommatophoca rossi*)
3. Crabeater Seal (*Lobodon carcinophagus*)
4. Leopard Seal (*Hydrurga leptonyx*)

ELEPHANT SEALS (2 species)

1. Northern Elephant Seal (*Mirounga angustirostris*)
2. Southern Elephant Seal (*Mirunga leonina*)

FAMILY: ODOBENIDAE (the Walruses)

WALRUS (1 species)

1. Walrus (*Odobenus rosmarus*)

OTHER BOOKS BY FRED BRUEMMER

1969   *The Long Hunt*

1971   *Seasons of the Eskimo*

1972   *Encounters with Arctic Animals*

1974   *The Arctic*

1977   *The Life of the Harp Seal*

1979   *Children of the North*

1980   *Summer at Bear River*

1985   *The Arctic World*

1986   *Arctic Animals*

1988   *Seasons of the Seal*

1989   *World of the Polar Bear*

1991   *Seals* (with Eric S. Grace)

1993   *Land of Dark, Land of Light* (with Karen Pandell)

1993   *Les Animaux du Grand Nord* (with Angèle Delaunois)

1993   *The Narwhal: Unicorn of the Sea*

1993   *Arctic Memories: Living with the Inuit*

1995   *Nanook and Nauja: The Polar Bear Cubs* (with Angèle Delaunois)

1995   *Kotik: The Baby Seal* (with Angèle Delaunois)

1997   *Polar Dance: Born of the North Wind* (with Tom Mangelsen)

INDEX